THE AUTHORS

JOHN BELLAMY FOSTER is editor of *Monthly Review* and professor emeritus of sociology at the University of Oregon. He has written many books including *Capitalism in the Anthropocene* and *The Return of Nature*, which won the Deutscher Memorial Prize.

VIJAY PRASHAD is the Executive Director of Tricontinental: Institute for Social Research. He is the author or editor of several books, including *Washington Bullets*, *The Darker Nations: A Biography of the Short-Lived Third World* and *The Poorer Nations: A Possible History of the Global South*. He is Chief Editor at LeftWord Books.

JOHN ROSS (Luo Siyi) is a senior fellow at Chongyang Institute for Financial Studies, Renmin University of China. He was formerly director of economic policy for the mayor of London.

DEBORAH VENEZIALE is a journalist and editor who has worked in the global supply chain sector for 35 years. She also collaborates as a researcher with Tricontinental: Institute for Social Research. She is currently living in Venice, Italy.

WASHINGTON'S NEW COLD WAR
A Socialist Perspective

by John Bellamy Foster, John Ross,
and Deborah Veneziale

Introduction by Vijay Prashad

This publication is issued under a Creative Commons Attribution-Non-commercial 4.0 International (CC BY-NC 4.0) license. The human-readable summary of the license is available at https://creativecommons.org/licenses/by-nc/4.0/.

ISBN 978-68590-000-7 paper
ISBN 978-68590-001-4 cloth
ISBN 978-68590-002-1 eBook

Typeset in Minion Pro and DIN condensed

MONTHLY REVIEW PRESS, NEW YORK
monthlyreview.org

5 4 3 2 1

Contents

Introduction by Vijay Prashad | 7

What Is Propelling the United States into Increasing
    International Military Aggression?
    by John Ross (Luo Siyi) | 12

Who Is Leading the United States to War?
    by Deborah Veneziale | 34

"Notes on Exterminism" for the Twenty-First Century
    Ecology and Peace Movements
    by John Bellamy Foster | 63

Notes | 87

Introduction

VIJAY PRASHAD

At the World Economic Forum meeting in Davos (Switzerland) on May 23, 2022, former U.S. Secretary of State Henry Kissinger made some remarks about Ukraine that struck a nerve. Rather than be caught up "in the mood of the moment," Kissinger said, the West—led by the United States—needs to enable a peace agreement that satisfies the Russians. "Pursuing the war beyond [this] point," Kissinger said, "would not be about the freedom of Ukraine, but a new war against Russia itself." Most of the commentary from the Western foreign policy establishment rolled their eyes and dismissed Kissinger's comments. Kissinger, no peacenik, nonetheless indicated the great danger of escalation toward not only the establishment of a new iron curtain around Asia but perhaps open—and lethal—warfare between the West and Russia as well as China. This sort of unthinkable outcome was too much, even for Henry Kissinger, whose boss, former President Richard Nixon, spoke frequently of the Madman Theory of international relations; Nixon told his chief of staff Bob Haldeman that he had his "hand on the nuclear button" to terrify Ho Chi Minh into capitulation.

During the lead-up to the U.S.'s illegal invasion of Iraq in 2003, I spoke to a senior member of the U.S. State Department who told me that the prevailing theory in Washington amounts to a simple slogan: *short-term pain for long-term gain*. He explained that the general view is that the nation's elites are willing to tolerate short-term pain for other countries—and perhaps for working people in the United States, who could experience economic difficulties due to the disruptions and carnage created by war. However, if all goes well, this price will result in long-term gain as the United States would be able to maintain what it has sought to maintain since the end of the Second World War, which is primacy. *If all goes well* is the premise that sent shivers down my back as he spoke, but what rattled me just as much was the callousness about who must face the pain and who would enjoy the gain. It was quite cynically said in Washington that it was worth the price that Iraqis and working-class U.S. soldiers be negatively impacted (and die), so long as large oil and financial companies could enjoy the fruits of a conquered Iraq. This attitude—*short term pain, long-term gain*— is the defining hallucination of the elites in the United States, who are unwilling to tolerate the project of building human dignity and the longevity of nature.

Short term pain, long-term gain defines the dangerous escalation by the United States and its Western allies against Russia and China. What is striking about the posture of the United States is that it seeks to prevent a historical process that seems inevitable, which is the process of Eurasian integration. After the collapse of the U.S. housing market and the major credit crisis in the Western banking sector, the Chinese government, alongside other Global South countries, pivoted to build platforms that were not dependent upon the markets of North America and Europe. These platforms included the creation of BRICS (Brazil, Russia, India, China, and South Africa) in 2009 and the announcement of One Belt, One Road (later the Belt and Road Initiative or BRI) in 2013. Russia's energy supply and its massive metal and mineral holdings, as well as China's industrial and technological capacity, drew many countries into association with the

BRI despite their political orientation, with Russia's export of energy undergirding this association. These countries included Poland, Italy, Bulgaria, and Portugal, while Germany is now China's largest trading partner in goods.

The historical fact of Eurasian integration threatened the primacy of the United States and of the Atlantic elites. It is this threat that drives the dangerous attempt by the United States to use any means to "weaken" both Russia and China. Old habits continue to dominate in Washington, which has long sought nuclear primacy to negate the theory of détente. The United States has developed a nuclear capacity and posture that would allow it to destroy the planet to maintain its hegemony. The strategies to weaken Russia and China include an attempt to isolate these countries through the escalation of the U.S.-imposed hybrid war (such as sanctions and the information war) and a desire to dismember these countries and then dominate them in perpetuity.

The three essays in this volume closely and rationally analyze the longer-term trends that have now manifested in Ukraine.

John Bellamy Foster, the editor of *Monthly Review*, catalogued the "escalation domination" theory of the U.S. establishment, which has been willing to risk nuclear winter—which means annihilation—to hold onto primacy. Despite the actual numbers of nuclear weapons held by Russia and the United States, the latter has developed an entire counterforce architecture that it believes can destroy Russian and Chinese nuclear weapons and then pulverize these countries into submission. This fantasy emerges not only in the turgid documents of U.S. policy makers, but it also appears occasionally in the popular press, where arguments are made about the importance of a nuclear attack against Russia.

Deborah Veneziale, a journalist based in Italy, excavates the social world of militarism in the United States, looking at how the various factions of the U.S. political elite have come together to support this strategy of confrontation against Russia and China. The intimate world of think tanks and arms production companies, of politicians and their scribes, has negated the constitutional protections of checks and balances. There is a rush to conflict so that the U.S. elites can protect their extraordinary control over global social wealth (the combined net worth of the richest 400 U.S. citizens is now close to $3.5 trillion, while the global elites, many of them from the United States, have hoarded nearly $40 trillion in illicit tax havens).

John Ross, a member of the No Cold War collective, writes that the United States has qualitatively escalated its military assault on the planet through the conflict in Ukraine. This war is dangerous because it shows that the United States is willing to directly confront Russia, a major power, and that it is willing to escalate its conflict with China by "Ukrainizing" Taiwan. What can constrain the United States, Ross argues, is China's resilience and its commitment to defending its sovereignty and its project, as well as the growing annoyance in the Global South against the U.S.'s imposition of its foreign policy objectives. Most countries in the world do not see the Ukraine War as their conflict since they are gripped with the need to address broader dilemmas of humanity. It is telling that the head of the African Union, Moussa Faki Mahamat, said on May 25, 2022, that Africa has become "the collateral victim of a distant conflict, that between Russia and Ukraine." The conflict is distant not only in terms of space, but also in terms of the political objectives of countries in Africa, as well as in Asia and Latin America.

This study is jointly produced by *Monthly Review*, No Cold War, and Tricontinental: Institute for Social Research. We invite you to read it, share it with friends, and discuss it whenever you get the opportunity. Precious human life and the longevity of the planet are at stake. It is impossible to ignore these facts. Most of the people of the world would like to get along with our real problems. We do not want to be dragooned into a conflict that is driven by a parochial desire by the Western elite to maintain their preponderant power. We affirm life.

What Is Propelling the United States into Increasing International Military Aggression?

JOHN ROSS

Introduction

The events leading to the Ukraine War represent a qualitative acceleration of a more than two-decade-long trend in which the United States has escalated its military aggression on an international level. Before the Ukraine War, the United States carried out military confrontations only against developing countries, which had far weaker armed forces and did not possess nuclear weapons: the bombing of Serbia in 1999, the invasions of Afghanistan in 2001 and of Iraq in 2003, and the bombing of Libya in 2011. However, the U.S. threat to extend the North Atlantic Treaty Organization (NATO) into Ukraine, which is the main cause of the war, represents something fundamentally different. The United States was aware that extending NATO into Ukraine would directly confront the national interests of Russia, a country with large military forces and an enormous nuclear arsenal. Though it would cross Russia's red lines, the United States was ready to take this risk.

The United States has not (yet) committed its own soldiers to the war in Ukraine, stating that this would threaten a world war and risk nuclear catastrophe. But it is, in fact, engaging in a proxy war against Russia. Not only has it insisted on leaving open the possibility that Ukraine could join NATO, but it trained Ukraine's army in the lead-up to the war and has now supplied massive amounts of military weapons and passed satellite and other intelligence information to the country. So far, U.S. aid to Ukraine has amounted to some $50 billion.

How the United States Pushed Ukraine into the War

The United States and its allies have been preparing Ukraine for war since at least 2014, such as by sending hundreds of instructors to train Ukraine's military. This is similar to its approach during the Gulf War in Iraq in 1990, reflecting a model that Washington appears to be using to achieve its geopolitical goals. Russia was purposefully lured into the situation in Ukraine beginning with the 2014 coup, when anti-Russian forces took power in Kiev, backed by Ukrainian neo-Nazis as well as by the United States. At that time, the Ukrainian army was not a powerful military force, having suffered considerably following the "reforms" launched in 1991, after the collapse of the Union of Socialist Soviet Republic (U.S.S.R.). Decades of neglect and underfunding led to decaying military infrastructure and equipment, along with the depletion of morale among officers and soldiers. As Vyacheslav Tetekin, a member of the Central Committee of the Communist Party of the Russian Federation (K.P.R.F.), puts it, "The Ukrainian army did not want [to] and could not fight."

After the 2014 coup, state spending was diverted away from improving social welfare and redeployed toward building up the military. From 2015–2019, Ukraine's military budget increased from $1.7 billion to $8.9 billion, constituting 6% of the country's GDP in 2019. Measured as a percentage of its GDP, Ukraine spent three times more on its military than most developed countries in the West. Extensive funds were poured into restoring and modernizing the country's military hardware, and ultimately reestablishing the military's combat capability.

During the 2014–15 war against Donbass (the Russian-speaking region of eastern Ukraine), Ukraine had little air combat support, as nearly all combat aircraft were in need of repair. However, by February 2022, the air force was equipped with approximately 150 fighters, bombers, and attack aircraft. The size of the Ukrainian armed forces also expanded dramatically. It is important to note that, at the end of 2021, remuneration for soldiers increased threefold, according to Tetekin's data. This strengthening of military power alongside powerful fortifications erected near Donbass indicates the U.S. intention to initiate conflict in the region.

However, despite these preparations for war, the Ukrainian army was unable to seriously contest with Russia. The balance of forces was clearly not in favor of Kiev. This did not matter to the United States, which sought to use Ukraine as cannon fodder against Russia. According to Tetekin, "the United States planned two options for the new, militarized Ukraine… The first one was to conquer Donbass and invade Crimea. The second option was to provoke Russia's armed intervention."

In December 2021, aware of the growing danger it faced from Ukraine under U.S. influence, Russia sought a set of security guarantees from NATO to defuse the crisis. In particular, Russia demanded that NATO end its eastward expansion, including membership of Ukraine. "The West…ignored these demands," Tetekin writes, "knowing that preparations for the invasion of Donbass [were] in full swing. Most combat-ready units of the Ukrainian Army, numbering up to 150 thousand people, were concentrated close to Donbass. They could break the resistance of local troops within days, with the complete destruction of Donetsk and Lugansk and [the] death of thousands."[1]

Ukraine Is a Qualitative Escalation of Military Aggression by the United States

It is therefore clear from both the fundamental political facts—the U.S.'s insistence on Ukraine's "right" to enter NATO—and the military facts—the U.S. buildup of Ukraine's armed forces—that the United States was preparing a confrontation in Ukraine, even though this would inevitably involve a direct clash with Russia. Consequently, in assessing the Ukraine crisis, it is important to note that the United States was prepared to escalate its military threats from simply those against developing countries—always unjust but not directly risking military conflicts with great powers or world wars—to aggression against very strong states such as Russia, which do risk global military conflict. Therefore, it is crucial to analyze what creates this escalating U.S. military aggression. Is it temporary, after which the United States will resume a more conciliatory course, or is increasing military escalation a long-term trend in U.S. policy?

This is, of course, of utmost importance for all countries, but particularly for China, itself a powerful state. To take only one key example, in parallel with escalating U.S. aggression against Russia, the United States has not merely imposed tariffs against China's economy and carried out a systematic international campaign to exploit the situation in Xinjiang for its own foreign policy agenda; it has also attempted to undermine the One China policy regarding Taiwan Province.

Among the United States' actions regarding Taiwan Province:

- For the first time since the commencement of United

States-China diplomatic relations, President Biden invited a representative of Taipei to the inauguration of a U.S. president.
- Speaker of the House of Representatives, Nancy Pelosi—the third-highest ranking U.S. official in order of presidential succession—visited Taipei on August 2, 2022.
- The United States has called for Taipei's participation in the UN.
- The United States has intensified sales of military armaments and equipment to the island.
- U.S. delegations visiting Taipei have increased.
- The United States has increased its military deployment in the South China Sea and has regularly sent U.S. warships through the Taiwan Strait.
- U.S. Special Operations Forces have trained Taiwanese ground troops as well as Taiwanese Navy sailors.

As is the case with Ukraine and Russia, the United States is fully conscious that the One China policy affects China's most fundamental national interests, and it has been the basis of U.S.-China relations for the fifty years since Nixon's 1972 visit to Beijing. To abandon it crosses China's red lines. It is therefore crystal clear that the United States is attempting in a confrontational way to undermine the One China policy in the same way that it deliberately decided to cross Russia's red lines in Ukraine.

Regarding the question of whether these U.S. provocations against both China and Russia are temporary, long term, or even permanent, the clear conclusion of this author is that the trend of U.S. military escalation will continue. However, given that such an issue, potentially involving wars, is of utmost seriousness and has extremely major practical consequences, exaggeration and mere propaganda are unacceptable. The aim here is therefore to present in a factual, objective, and calm way the reasons why the United States will attempt to further escalate its military aggression over the coming period. In addition, I will ascertain which trends may serve to counteract this dangerous U.S. policy and which may exacerbate it.

The Economic and Military Position of the United States during the "Old Cold War" and the "New Cold War"

Reduced to the most essential facts, the key forces that have driven this escalating U.S. policy of military aggression, which has now lasted more than two decades, are clear. They are, first, the permanent loss of the overwhelming weight of the U.S. economy in global production, and, second, the preponderance of U.S. military power and spending. This asymmetry creates a very dangerous period for humanity, one in which the U.S. may attempt to compensate for its relative economic decline through its use of military force. This helps explain U.S. military attacks on developing countries, as well as its escalating confrontation with Russia in Ukraine. An important question is whether this U.S. military aggression will increase further to include a growing confrontation with China, even to the point of a willingness to consider a world war. To answer this question, it is necessary to make an accurate analysis of the United States' economic and military situation.

To start with the economy, in 1950, near the commencement of the first Cold War, the United States accounted for 27.3 percent of the world GDP. In comparison, the U.S.S.R., the largest socialist economy of that period, accounted for 9.6 percent of world GDP. In other words, the U.S. economy was nearly three times larger than the Soviet economy.[2] During the entire post–Second World War period (the first Cold War), the U.S.S.R. never came close to the U.S.'s GDP, equaling only 44.4 percent of it in 1975. That is, even at the peak of the U.S.S.R.'s relative economic achievement, the

U.S. economy was still more than twice the size of the Soviet economy. Throughout the "Old Cold War" the United States enjoyed a significant economic lead over the U.S.S.R., at least in terms of conventional measures of output.

Turning to the present situation, the United States accounts for considerably less of the global GDP than it did in 1950, ranging from roughly 15 to 25 percent depending on how it is measured. China, the main economic rival of the United States today, has gotten much closer to parity with the U.S. economy. Even at market exchange rates, which oscillate somewhat independently of actual outputs with currency fluctuations, China's GDP is already 74 percent that of the United States', a far higher level than the U.S.S.R. ever achieved. Furthermore, China's economic growth rate has for some time been much faster than that of the United States, meaning that it will continue to close in on the latter.

Calculated in purchasing power parities (PPPs, which account for countries' different price levels), the measure used by Angus Maddison and the IMF, by 2021, the United States accounted for only 16 percent of the world economy— that is, 84 percent of the world economy is outside of the United States. By the same measure, China's economy is already 18 percent larger than that of the United States. By 2026, according to International Monetary Fund PPP projections, China's economy will be at least 35 percent larger than that of the United States. The economic gap between China and the United States is far closer than anything the U.S.S.R. ever achieved.

Taking into account other factors, no matter how they are measured, China has become by far the world's largest manufacturing power. In 2019, the latest available data point, China accounted for 28.7 percent of world manufacturing production, compared to 16.8 percent for the United States. In other words, China's global share of manufacturing production was more than 70 percent higher than that of the United States. The U.S.S.R., on the other hand, never came close to overtaking the United States in manufacturing production.

Turning to trade in goods, the defeat of the United States by China in the trade war launched by Trump is even somewhat humiliating for him and the country. In 2018, China already traded more goods than any other country, though its trade in goods was only around 10 percent larger than that of the United States at that time. By 2021, China's trade in goods outpaced the U.S. by 31 percent. The situation was even worse for the United States in terms of the export of goods: in 2018, China's exports were 58 percent higher than those of the U.S., and, by 2021, China's exports were 91 percent higher. In summary, not only has China become by far the world's largest goods-trading nation, but the United States has suffered a clear defeat in the trade war launched by the Trump and Biden administrations.

Even more fundamental from a macroeconomic viewpoint is China's lead in savings (household, business, and state), the source of real capital investment and the driving force of economic growth. According to the latest available data in 2019, China's gross capital savings were, in absolute terms, 56 percent higher than those of the United States—the equivalent of $6.3 trillion, compared to $4.03 trillion. However, this figure greatly understates China's lead: once depreciation is taken into account, China's net annual capital creation was 635 percent higher than that of the United States—the equivalent of $3.9 trillion, compared to $0.6 trillion. In summary, China is greatly adding to its capital stock each year, while the United States, in comparative terms, is adding little.

The net result of these trends is that China has overwhelmingly outperformed the United States in terms of economic growth, not merely in the entire four-decade period since 1978, as is well known, but continuing into the recent period.

In inflation adjusted prices, since 2007 (the year before the international financial crisis), the U.S. economy has grown by 24 percent, while China's economy has grown by 177 percent—that is, China's economy has grown more than seven times faster than the U.S. economy. On the terrain of relatively peaceful competition, China is winning.[3]

The U.S. lead in productivity, technology, and company size means that, overall, its economy is still stronger than China's, but the gap between the two countries is far narrower than was the case between the United States and the U.S.S.R. Furthermore, whatever one might say are the exact relative economic strengths of the two global giants, it is clear that the United States has lost its global economic predominance. From a purely economic standpoint, we are already in a global era of multipolarity.

The U.S. Military in a Moment of Economic Decline

These economic setbacks for the United States have led some, particularly in a few circles in the West, to believe that the defeat of the United States is inevitable or has already occurred. A similar view has been expressed by a small number of people in China who take the view that China's comprehensive strength has already overtaken that of the United States. These views are incorrect. They forget, in V. I. Lenin's famous words, that "politics must take precedence over economics, that is the ABC of Marxism," and, regarding politics, that "political power grows out of the barrel of a gun," in the famous dictum of Chairman Mao. The fact that the United States is losing its economic superiority does not mean that it will simply allow this economic trend to peacefully continue: to presume that this is the case would be to make the mistake of placing economics before politics. On the contrary, the fact that the United States is losing ground economically both to China and to other countries is pushing it toward military and military-related political means to overcome the consequences of its economic defeats.

More precisely, the danger to all countries is that the United States has not lost military supremacy. In fact, U.S. military spending is greater than that of the next nine countries combined. Only in one area, nuclear weapons, is U.S. strength roughly equaled by another country, Russia, which is due to Russia's inheritance of nuclear weapons from the U.S.S.R. The exact numbers of nuclear weapons held by countries in general are state secrets, but, as of 2022, according to a leading Western estimate by the Federation of American Scientists, Russia possesses 5,977 nuclear weapons, while the United States has 5,428. Russia and the United States each have about 1,600 active deployed strategic nuclear warheads (though the United States has far more nuclear weapons than China).[4] Meanwhile, in the field of conventional weapons, U.S. spending is far greater than that of any other country.

This divergence in the United States' position in economic and military spheres underlies its aggressive policy and creates the distinction between its economic and military positions in the present "New Cold War" compared to the "Old Cold War" waged against the U.S.S.R. In the Old Cold War, U.S. and U.S.S.R. military strengths were approximately equal, but, as already noted, the U.S. economy was much larger. Therefore, in the Old Cold War, the U.S. strategy was to attempt to shift issues onto an economic terrain. Even Reagan's military buildup in the 1980s was not intended to be used to wage war against the U.S.S.R., but rather to engage it in an arms race that would damage the Soviet economy. Consequently, despite tension, the Cold War never turned to a hot war. The U.S.'s present situation is the opposite: its relative economic position has weakened tremendously, but its military power is great. Therefore, it attempts to move issues to the military terrain, which explains its escalating military aggression and why this is a permanent trend.

This means that humanity has entered a very dangerous period. The United States might be losing in peaceful economic competition, but it still retains a military lead over China. The temptation is then for the United States to use "direct" and "indirect" military means to attempt to halt China's development.

The Direct and Indirect Use of U.S. Military Strength

The U.S. employs both "direct" and "indirect" means to display its military strength, which are far more expansive than the most extreme "direct" possibility of a frontal war against China. Some of these approaches are already in use, while others are being discussed. The former includes, for example:

- subordinating other countries to the U.S. military and attempting to pressure these countries to adopt more hostile economic policies toward China, as is the case in relation to Germany and the European Union.
- attempting to overcome the multipolar economic character of the world, which has already been established, instead creating alliances dominated in a unilateral way by the United States. This is clearly the case with NATO, the Quad (United States, Japan, Australia, India), and in relation to some other nations.
- attempting to force countries that have good economic relations with China to weaken these relations. This is particularly evident with Australia and is now being attempted elsewhere.

Meanwhile, approaches that are being discussed include the possibility of waging wars against allies of China and Russia and attempting to draw China into a "limited" war with the United States regarding Taiwan Province.

An example of the U.S.'s integrated use of both direct and

indirect military pressure was given by *Financial Times* chief U.S. political commentator, Janan Ganesh, following the outbreak of the war in Ukraine, who explained how "America will be the ultimate 'winner' of the Ukrainian crisis." Within three days of Russia's intervention in Ukraine, Ganesh writes, Germany expedited the construction of the country's first two liquefied natural gas (LNG) terminals. By 2026, the U.S. will likely become Germany's top LNG supplier, as it is closer both geographically and politically, thereby eliminating German dependence on Russian energy imports. Ganesh also argues that Germany's pledge to increase its defense budget will also benefit the U.S. because Germany would in turn "share more of NATO's financial and logistical burden" that is currently held by the U.S. Lastly, he points to what could be a massive advance for the U.S.:

> A Europe that is more tethered to America and at the same time less of a drain on it: no Kissinger could have schemed what the Kremlin is poised to achieve through accident. Far from ending the US turn to Asia, the war in Ukraine might be the event that enables it.
>
> As for that part of the world, if the Chinese aim is to exorcise at least the Pacific Rim of US influence, the past six weeks have been an education in the size of the task. Japan could hardly be doing more to side with Kyiv, and therefore with Washington.[5]

In short, the United States used its military pressure to increase the economic subordination of Germany and Japan. Though many other variants can be envisaged, their common feature is that the United States uses its military strength to attempt to compensate for its weakened economic position. Understood in this way, it is clear that the United States has already embarked on this fundamental policy of directly and indirectly using its military strength.

Since China is experiencing more rapid economic development than the United States, it is likely that its military strength will eventually become its equal. However, it would take years for China to build a nuclear arsenal equivalent to that of the United States, even if China decided to embark on such a policy. It would likely take even longer to create conventional armaments equivalent to those of the United States given the enormous technological development and training of personnel required for such advanced air and naval forces and much else. Therefore, the United States will have stronger armed forces than China for a very significant number of years, creating the permanent temptation for the United States to attempt to use military means to compensate for its declining economic position.

The Significance of the War in Ukraine

Two fundamental lessons can be drawn from the events leading to the war in Ukraine.

First, it confirms that it is pointless to ask the United States for compassion. After the U.S.S.R.'s dissolution in 1991, for seventeen years Russia pursued a policy of attempting to have friendly relations with the United States. Under Boris Yeltsin, Russia was humiliatingly subordinated to the United States. During the early period of Putin's presidency, Russia gave direct assistance to the United States in its so-called war on terror and in the U.S. invasion of Afghanistan. The U.S. response was to violate every promise it had made that NATO would not advance "by an inch" toward Russia, all while aggressively increasing military pressure on Russia.

Second, this dynamic makes it clear that the outcome of the war in Ukraine is crucial not only for Russia, but also for China and for the entire world. Russia is the only country which is the United States' equal in terms of nuclear weapons, and the good relations between China and Russia are a major deterrent for the U.S. not to adopt any policy of a direct attack on China. The aim of the U.S. in Ukraine is precisely to attempt to bring about a fundamental change in Russia's policy and install a government in Moscow which no longer defends Russia's national interests—and one which is hostile to China and subordinate to the U.S. If that were achieved, not only would China face a greatly increased military threat from the U.S., but its long northern border with Russia would become a strategic threat; China would be surrounded from the north. In other words, both Russia and China's national interests would be undermined. In the words of Sergei Glazyev, a Russian commissioner on the executive body of the Eurasian Economic Union: "After failing to weaken China head-on through a trade war, the Americans shifted the main blow to Russia, which they see as a weak link in the global geopolitics and economy. The Anglo-Saxons are trying to implement their eternal Russophobic ideas to destroy our country, and at the same time to weaken China, because the strategic alliance of the Russian Federation and the PRC is too tough for the United States."[6]

U.S. Military Actions and the Constraints They Face

As the United States is pushed both by its declining economic position and by its military strength, there is no limit on an "internal" (domestic) level to the scope of U.S. aggression. History clearly shows that the U.S. has been prepared to carry out the most extremely violent military aggression to the point of being willing to destroy entire countries. In one of many examples, in the Korean War, the U.S. destroyed nearly all of North Korea's cities and towns, including an estimated 85 percent of its buildings.

The U.S. bombing in Indochina during the Vietnam War was even greater in scale, using both explosive devices and chemical weapons, such as the notorious Agent Orange, which produces horrifying deformities. From 1964 to August 15, 1973, the United States Air Force dropped over six million tons of bombs and other ordnance in Indochina, while U.S. Navy and Marine Corps aircraft expended another 1.5 million tons in Southeast Asia. As Micheal Clodfelter notes in *The Limits of Air Power:*

> This tonnage far exceeded that expended in World War II and in the Korean War. The U.S. Air Force consumed 2,150,000 tons of munitions in World War II and in the Korean War—1,613,000 tons in the European theater and 537,000 tons in the Pacific theater—and 454,000 tons in the Korean War.[7]

Edward Miguel and Gerard Roland expand upon the same point in their study on the long-term impact of bombing in Vietnam, noting that:

> Vietnam War bombing thus represented at least three times as much (by weight) as both European and Pacific theater World War II bombing combined, and about fifteen times the total tonnage in the Korean War. Given the prewar Vietnamese population of approximately 32 million, U.S. bombing translates into hundreds of kilograms of explosives per capita during the conflict. For another comparison, the atomic bombs dropped at Hiroshima and Nagasaki had the power of roughly 15,000 and 20,000 tons of TNT. . . . U.S. bombing in Indochina represents 100 times the combined impact of the Hiroshima and Nagasaki atomic bombs.[8]

In the invasion of Iraq, the United States was prepared to (and did) devastate the country, using horrific weapons such as depleted uranium, which is still producing terrible birth defects many years after the U.S. attack. In its bombing of Libya in 2011, the United States reduced what had been one of the richest income per capita countries in Africa, with a developed welfare state, to a society in which tribal conflicts exist and in which slaves are openly sold. The list goes on.

In short, the evidence shows that there is no level of crime or atrocity to which the United States is not prepared to descend. If the United States were to posit that it could eliminate the economic challenge from China by launching an atomic war, there is no evidence that it would not do so. Furthermore, while there are certainly anti-war movements in the United States, they are nowhere near strong enough to prevent the United States from using nuclear weapons if it were to decide to do so. There are no adequate internal constraints in the U.S. that could prevent it from launching a war against China.

But if there are no fundamental internal constraints on U.S. aggression, there are certainly great external constraints. The first is other countries' possession of nuclear weapons. That is why the explosion of China's first nuclear bomb in 1964 is rightly regarded as a great national achievement. China's possession of nuclear weapons is a fundamental deterrent to a nuclear attack by the United States. Nevertheless, unlike its adversary, China has a No First Use nuclear weapons policy, showing its restraint and defensive military posture.

A full-scale nuclear war involving the United States, China, and Russia would be a military catastrophe without precedent in human history. In such a war, at a minimum hundreds of millions would die. It would be infinitely preferable to prevent the escalation of U.S. military aggression before it reached that point, but what are the chances of doing so?

The overall trend of United States policy since the Second World War shows a clear and logical pattern. When the United States feels that it is in a strong position, its policy is aggressive; when it feels weakened, it becomes more conciliatory.

This was shown most dramatically before, during, and after the Vietnam War, but also in other periods.

Immediately after the Second World War, the United States considered itself to be—and was—in a strong position and was therefore prepared to carry out a war against Korea. Even after the U.S. failed to win the Korean War, it still felt confident enough to attempt to diplomatically isolate China during the 1950s and 1960s, depriving the country of a seat at the UN, blocking direct diplomatic relations, and so on. However, the United States suffered severe defeats due to the failure of its war on Vietnam, in which it sought to defeat the Vietnamese people's national liberation struggle and the large-scale military support they received from China and the U.S.S.R. The weakening of the United States' global position as a result of its defeat in Vietnam (beginning even before the official end of the war in 1975) led it to adopt a more conciliatory policy, symbolized by Nixon's 1972 visit to Beijing and followed by the establishment of full diplomatic relations with China. Soon after 1972, the United States opened a policy of détente with the U.S.S.R. However, by the 1980s, having regrouped and recovered from defeat in Vietnam, the United States returned to a more aggressive policy toward the U.S.S.R. under then President Ronald Reagan.

This same pattern of U.S. aggression in moments of strength or a more conciliatory attitude in moments of weakness can also be seen around the international financial crisis that began in 2007/8. This crisis dealt a severe blow to the U.S. economy, as a result of which the United States began to emphasize international cooperation. Though the G20, which includes the world's largest economies and two-thirds of its population, was established in 1999, it only began to hold yearly meetings after the 2007/8 economic crisis. In 2009, the G20 group pledged itself as the major force for international economic and financial cooperation, with the United States playing a major role. In particular, as it felt weakened, the United States displayed a more cooperative attitude toward China in these areas.

As the United States recovered from the international financial crisis, its posture with respect to China became increasingly aggressive, culminating in the launch of Trump's trade war against the country. That is, as soon as the United States felt itself stronger, it became aggressive.

A Comparison of Today's Reality and the Pre-Second World War Period

Turning to an historical comparison, we can juxtapose the present situation with the period leading up to the Second World War. The immediate path to that war began with the strengthening of Japanese militarism and the resulting invasion of Northeast China in 1931, followed by Hitler's ascension to power in Germany in 1933. Yet, despite these ominous events, the war was not inevitable. The first victories of Japanese militarism and German fascism escalated to world war as a result of a series of the Allied powers' defeats and capitulations between 1931 and 1939 as well as their failure to confront the Japanese militarists and German Nazis.

The ruling political party in China, the Kuomintang, concentrated its efforts for most of the 1930s not on repelling Japan but on fighting the communists. Meanwhile, the United States failed to intervene to stop Japan until it was itself attacked at Pearl Harbor in 1941. In Europe, Britain and France failed to stop the remilitarization of Nazi Germany even when they had the right to do so under the Treaty of Versailles. Further, they did not support the legitimate government of Spain in 1936 against the fascist coup and civil war launched by Francisco Franco, who was supported by Hitler. Then, they directly capitulated to Hitler's dismemberment of Czechoslovakia under the notorious Munich Pact of 1938.

Today, we see a pattern similar to 1931, which marked the beginning of the lead-up to the Second World War. Though support for an aggressive world war certainly does not have majority support in the United States, such support does exist among a small and, so far, fringe element within the U.S. foreign policy/military establishment. If the United States suffers political defeats, it will not move directly to frontal war with China or Russia. Nonetheless, the medium-term danger exists that—as was the case following Japan's invasion of China in 1931 and Hitler's coming to power in 1933—if the United States achieves victories in more limited struggles, it will likely be encouraged to move toward a major global military conflict. The decisive struggle must be to prevent such a global conflict. This means that it is of utmost importance that the United States does not win immediate struggles, such as the war it provoked in Ukraine, its attempt to undermine the One China policy with regard to Taiwan, and its economic wars against many other countries.

The Main Forces Opposing U.S. Military Aggression

There are two powerful forces that oppose U.S. military aggression. The first, and most powerful, is China, whose economic development is not merely crucial for improving the living standards of its population, but also for eventually allowing the country to put its military forces more on par with those of the United States. This will very likely be the ultimate deterrent to U.S. military aggression. The second powerful force is the opposition of a large number of countries to U.S. aggression—including many in the Global South, comprising the majority of the world's people—not merely from a moral viewpoint but from direct self-interest. The U.S's attempt to overcome the consequences of its economic failures by military and political means inevitably leads it to take actions against numerous other countries' interests.

One among many examples of the impacts of these actions is that the U.S. provocation of the war in Ukraine has helped create a massive increase in world food prices because Russia and Ukraine are the world's largest international suppliers of wheat and fertilizer. Meanwhile, banning the Chinese telecommunications company Huawei from participation in 5G telecommunications development means that the inhabitants of every country that agrees to the U.S. ban pays more for their telecommunications. U.S. pressure to force Germany to buy U.S. liquefied natural gas, instead of Russian natural gas, raises energy prices in Germany. In Latin America, the United States attempts to prevent countries from pursuing policies of national independence. U.S. tariffs on China's exports raises the cost of living for U.S. households. The fact that, in practice, other countries' populations are being forced to finance aggressive U.S. militarism is bound to generate opposition to such policies and their outcomes.

These two mutually reinforcing forces—China's own development and the fact that U.S. policy is against the interests of the overwhelming majority of the world's population—constitute the main obstacles to U.S. aggression. Integrating China's development with the international forces that are opposed to the U.S.'s attacks against them is therefore the most crucial task for the majority of the global population. While those of us outside of the country cannot fully grasp the complexities facing China's leaders, we can say that they shoulder a great responsibility not only to push the world toward peace and a sustainable planet, but also to make good on the promises of their revolution and to justify the great sacrifices of peasants and workers—the very sacrifices that made China's current standing in the world possible.

The Choices Facing the United States

The U.S. turn to escalating military aggression alongside its loss of economic supremacy has already begun. In Ukraine, the United States is directly and forcefully challenging Russia, a state with powerful atomic weapons, thereby raising a potential risk of a nuclear war. Simultaneously, it is applying maximum pressure on its allies, such as Germany, to damage their own interests by subordinating themselves to U.S. policy.

However, the United States is still hesitant to utilize full military force, evidently weighing the gains and risks of escalating its military aggression. Though the United States provoked the Ukraine War by threatening to extend NATO into the country, thereby giving it access to ever more deadly weaponry and intelligence, it has not yet dared to directly commit its military forces to this war, showing that there is still considerable uncertainty at work at the highest levels of the U.S. state machinery.

All of this directly affects Russia and China's relations with each other, and it makes the outcome of the war in Ukraine crucial for the entire world. Because friendly Sino-Russian relations pose a formidable economic and military obstacle to U.S. threats of war, the central strategic goal of U.S. policy is to separate Russia and China. If this can be achieved, then the United States will have a greater capacity to attack them individually, including through the use of its military strength.

Conclusion

The United States will increase its aggressive actions toward China, as well as toward other countries, not only in the economic field but in particular through the direct and indirect use of U.S. military power, hesitating only when it suffers defeats. Naturally, every opening to develop a conciliatory approach by the United States must be taken advantage of, but it is essential to be clear that U.S. policy during such periods, when it has suffered defeats, will attempt to regroup its forces to launch a new aggressive policy.

Defeating U.S. aggression depends in large part on the overall domestic development of China in the economic, military, and all other fields, which is also in the interests of other countries suffering from U.S. aggression. After China's own domestic development, the most important force blocking U.S. aggression is the opposition of the majority of the world's population and countries whose position is worsened by U.S. policy. The degree to which U.S. military-based aggression, both direct and indirect, will intensify depends on how much the United States is defeated in individual struggles. The more it is successful, the more aggressive it will become; the more it is weakened, the more conciliatory it will become.

In the short term, the outcome of the war in Ukraine will therefore be crucial for the broader geopolitical reality. While the details of U.S. aggressive foreign policy cannot be seen with a crystal ball, the overall escalation of U.S. aggression clearly follows from its combination of economic weakening and military strength unless it suffers significant defeats.

Who Is Leading the United States to War?

DEBORAH VENEZIALE

The world is sensing the United States' growing rapacious intent for war.[1] Amid the development of the Ukraine crisis, the United States and NATO have been attempting to escalate their proxy war with Russia while continuing to intensify their siege and provocations against China. This intent to go to war was on display during the May 15, 2022, segment of NBC's *Meet the Press*, which simulated a U.S. war against China.[2] It should be noted that this "war game" was organized by the Center for a New American Security (CNAS), a prominent Washington, D.C., think tank that is funded by the U.S. and allied governments, including the Taipei Economic and Cultural Representative Office, George Soros's Open Society Foundations, and an array of U.S. military and technology companies such as Raytheon, Lockheed Martin, Northrop Grumman, General Dynamics, Boeing, Facebook, Google, and Microsoft.[3]

This simulation is in line with other alarming signals toward war from both Congress and the Pentagon. On April 5, Charles Richard, commander of U.S. Strategic Command, made a case before Congress that Russia and China pose nuclear threats to the United States, claiming that China is likely to use nuclear coercion for its own benefit.[4] Shortly thereafter, on April 14, a bipartisan delegation of U.S. lawmakers visited Taiwan. On May 5, South Korea announced that it had joined a cyber defense organization under NATO.

In June, at its annual summit, NATO named Russia its "most significant and direct threat" and singled out China as a "challenge [to] our interests." Furthermore, South Korea, Japan, Australia, and New Zealand participated in the summit for the first time, which suggests the possibility that an Asian branch may be formed in the future. Finally, on August 2, in a blatant provocation of Beijing, U.S. House of Representatives Speaker Nancy Pelosi—the third-highest ranking official in the Biden administration—visited Taiwan, escorted by the U.S. Air Force.[5]

In the face of the Biden administration's aggressive foreign policy, one can't help but wonder: among the U.S. ruling elite, who is advocating war? Is there a mechanism to curb such belligerence in the country?

This article comes to three conclusions. First, in the Biden administration, two elite foreign policy groups that used to compete against each other—liberal hawks and neoconservatives—have merged strategically, forming the most important foreign policy consensus within the country's elite echelon since 1948 and bringing U.S. war policy to a new level. Second, in consideration of its long-term interests, the big bourgeoisie in the United States has reached a consensus that China is a strategic rival, and it has established solid support for this foreign policy. Third, the so-called democratic institutions of checks and balances are completely incapable of restraining this belligerent policy from spreading due to the design of the U.S. Constitution, the expansion of far-right forces, and the sheer monetization of elections.

The Merging of Belligerent Foreign Policy Elites

Early representatives of U.S. liberal interventionism included Democratic presidents such as Harry Truman, John F. Kennedy, and Lyndon B. Johnson, whose ideological roots can be traced back to Woodrow Wilson's notion that America should stand on the world stage fighting for democracy. The invasion of Vietnam was guided by this ideology.

After the U.S. defeat in Vietnam, the Democratic Party temporarily reduced calls for intervention as part of its foreign policy. However, Democratic Senator Henry "Scoop" Jackson (also known at the time as "the senator from Boeing"), a liberal hawk, joined with other anti-communists and staunch interventionists, helping to inspire the neoconservative movement. The neoconservatives, including a number of Jackson's supporters and former staffers, supported Republican Ronald Reagan in the late 1970s because of his commitment to confront alleged Soviet expansionism.

With the dissolution of the Soviet Union in 1991 and the rise of U.S. unilateralism, the neoconservatives entered the mainstream in U.S. foreign policy with their thought leader, Paul Wolfowitz, who had been a former aide to Henry Jackson. In 1992, just a few months after the disintegration of the Soviet Union, Wolfowitz, then undersecretary of defense for policy, introduced his *Defense Policy Guidance*, which explicitly advocated for the United States to maintain a permanent unipolar position. This would be realized, he explained, through the expansion of U.S. military power into the former Soviet Union's sphere of influence and along all its perimeters with the object of preventing the reemergence of Russia as a great power. The U.S.-led unipolar strategy, implemented through the projection of military force, guided the foreign policies of George H.W. Bush and his son George W. Bush, as well as Bill Clinton and Barack Obama. The U.S. was able to launch the first Gulf War in large part due to Soviet weakness. This was followed by the U.S. and NATO's military dismemberment of Yugoslavia. After 9/11, the Bush Jr. administration's foreign policy was completely dominated by the neoconservatives, including Vice President Dick Cheney and Defense Secretary Donald Rumsfeld.

While both liberal hawks and neoconservatives have

ardently advocated for foreign military interventions, historically there have been two important differences between them. First, liberal hawks tended to believe that the United States should influence the United Nations and other international institutions to carry out military intervention, while neoconservatives tended to ignore multilateral institutions. Second, liberal hawks sought to lead military interventions alongside Western allies, while neoconservatives were more willing to conduct unilateral military operations and flagrantly violate international law. As Niall Ferguson, a historian at Harvard University, put it, the neoconservatives were happy to accept the title of the American Empire and unilaterally decide to attack any country as the world's hegemonic power.[6]

Although Republicans and Democrats have historically developed their own policy and advocacy institutions, it is a misconception to think that they have distinct approaches to foreign policy strategy. It is true that think tanks such as the Heritage Foundation are major neoconservative strongholds that have leaned toward Republican policy, while others such as the Brookings Institution and the later established CNAS have been home to more pro-Democratic liberal hawks. However, members of both parties have worked in each of these organizations, with differences centering around specific policy proposals, not partisan affiliation. In reality, behind the White House and Congress, a bipartisan policy planning network consisting of nonprofit foundations, universities, think tanks, research groups, and other institutions collectively shape the agendas of corporations and capitalists into policy proposals and reports.

Another common misconception is that the so-called progressive side of liberalism will promote social development, provide international assistance, and limit military spending. However, the neoliberal period, which began in the mid-1970s, has been characterized by the state's subordination to market forces and austerity in social spending in areas such as healthcare, food assistance, and education, all while encouraging unlimited military spending, severely damaging the quality of life for the vast majority of the population. Both Republicans and Democrats follow the principles of neoliberalism, as exemplified by Biden's annual budget for 2022, which includes a 4 percent increase in military spending, and the fact that, during the COVID-19 pandemic, $1.7 trillion of the $5 trillion that the U.S. government provided in stimulus funding went directly into the pockets of corporations.[7] Neoliberalism has had a particularly devastating impact in the Global South, where it has dragged developing countries into debt traps and coerced them into endless debt payments to the International Monetary Fund and the World Bank.

In the field of foreign policy, the most influential U.S. think tank since the Second World War has been the Council on Foreign Relations (CFR), which is funded by an array of ruling class sources. Founder-level corporate members of the council include leaders in energy (Chevron, ExxonMobil, Hess, Tellurian), finance (Bank of America, BlackRock, Citi, Goldman Sachs, JPMorgan Chase, Morgan Stanley, Moody's, Nasdaq), technology (Accenture, Apple, AT&T, Cisco), and the internet (Google, Meta), among other sectors, and the CFR's current board includes Richard Haass, Bush Sr.'s principal adviser on the Middle East, and Ashton Carter, Obama's secretary of defense. The German magazine *Der Spiegel* described the CFR as "the most influential private institution in the United States and the Western world" and "the politburo for capitalism," while Richard Harwood, former senior editor and ombudsman at the *Washington Post*, called the council and its members "the nearest thing we have to a ruling establishment in the United States."[8] The CFR's policy proposals reflect the long-term strategic thinking of the U.S. bourgeoisie, as seen by its proposal to "strengthen

U.S.-Japan coordination in response to the Taiwan issue" in January 2022, ahead of Pelosi's visit to Taiwan in August of the same year.

Regardless of which party's candidates the staffers of these various institutions support in the elections, this long-standing bipartisan, collaborative network has maintained consistent foreign policy in Washington. This network promotes a U.S. supremacist worldview that denies other countries' right to be involved in international affairs, an ideology dating back to the 1823 Monroe Doctrine that proclaimed U.S. domination over the entire Western hemisphere. Today's U.S. foreign policy elite has extended the doctrine's application from the Americas to the entire world. Cross-party synergy and party switching are common for this group of foreign policy makers, which is closely tied to the ruling capitalist class and its surrogates within the political power elite that control U.S. foreign policy, as well as to the Deep State (the intelligence services together with the military).

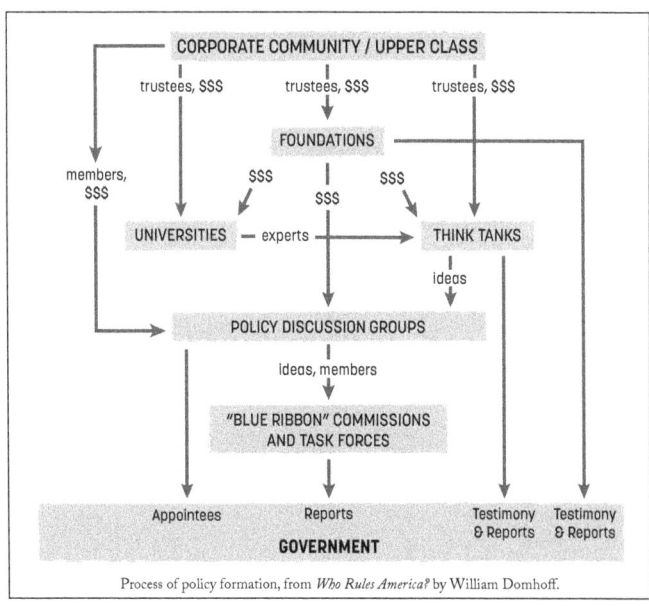

Process of policy formation, from *Who Rules America?* by William Domhoff.

At the turn of the century, neoconservatives, who gathered in the Republican Party, were more concerned with the disintegration and denuclearization of Russia than they were with China. Around 2008, however, forces within the U.S. political elite began to realize that China's economy would continue its strong rise and that its future leaders would not cave to U.S. influence; there would be no Chinese equivalent of Gorbachev or Yeltsin. Beginning in this period, the neoconservatives began to take an entirely confrontational approach to China and pursue containment. At the same time, some pro-Democratic liberal hawks founded CNAS, and Hillary Clinton, then secretary of state, led the development and implementation of the Pivot to Asia, a strategic shift in U.S. foreign policy that was applauded by the neoconservatives, who were still in the Republican camp at the time. Clinton was hailed as a "strong voice" by Max Boot, a political commentator and senior fellow at CFR, who, in 2003, wrote that, "[g]iven the historical baggage that 'imperialism' carries, there's no need for the U.S. government to embrace the term. But it should definitely embrace the practice."[9] Today, extending NATO to Ukraine and confronting Russia remains a priority for neoconservatives and liberal hawks alike. Both groups disagree with the realists who propose a détente with Russia in order to strengthen the confrontation with China.

However, the election of Trump in 2016 briefly created turbulence in the CFR consensus. As John Bellamy Foster wrote in *Trump in the White House: Tragedy and Farce*, the former president rose to power partly through the mobilization of a neofascist movement based in the white lower-middle class.[10] Only a small number of people in the big capital elite supported him initially. Among them were Dick Uihlein, the owner of the shipping giant Uline; Bernie Marcus, the founder of the building materials retailer Home Depot; Robert Mercer, an investor in the far-right media outlet Breitbart News

Network; and Timothy Mellon, grandson of the banking tycoon Andrew Mellon. Trump's tendency to shrink engagement in global affairs—as seen with the withdrawal of troops from Syria and the initiation of the withdrawal from Afghanistan as well as diplomatic contact with North Korea—favored the short-term interests of the lower and middle bourgeoisie and won the support of foreign policy realists, including Henry Kissinger, but it upset the neoconservatives. A group of elite neoconservatives played a major role in the campaign against Trump, with some 300 officials who had supported the Bush administration backing the Democratic Party in the 2020 election. This included the aforementioned Boot, who has become a thought leader on foreign policy and has had a strong impact on the Biden administration.

Under Biden, the CFR consensus resumed, and the neoconservatives and liberal hawks have become completely aligned on the country's strategic orientation. Their joint awareness of China's rise has fostered a unity between these two groups unseen in decades. This unity is based on the theory of international affairs that stipulates that the United States should actively intervene in other countries' politics, make every effort to promote "freedom and democracy," crack down on those states that challenge Western economic and military dominance, remove unwanted governments, and secure global hegemony by all means—with Russia and China as its primary targets. In May 2021, Secretary of State Antony Blinken (who previously served as deputy secretary of state under Obama) declared that the U.S. would defend an ambiguous "rules-based international order," a term that refers to U.S.-dominated international and security organizations rather than broader UN-based institutions. Blinken's stance suggests that, under the Biden administration, liberal hawks have officially forsaken the pretense of following the UN or other international multilateral organizations unless they bow to U.S. diktat.

In 2019, the prominent neoconservative Robert Kagan co-authored an article with Antony Blinken urging the United States to abandon Trump's America First policy. They called for the containment (i.e., siege and weakening) of Russia and China and proposed a policy of "preventive diplomacy and deterrence" against America's adversaries, that is, troops and tanks wherever it is deemed necessary.[11] Incidentally, Kagan's wife, Victoria Nuland, served as the assistant secretary of state for European and Eurasian affairs in the Obama administration. Nuland played a key role in organizing and supporting the 2014 color revolution/coup in Ukraine and has boasted about the billions of dollars the United States has spent to "promote democracy" in the country.[12] She is currently serving as undersecretary of state for political affairs in the Biden administration, the third-highest position in the State Department after Secretary Blinken and Deputy Secretary Wendy Sherman. She is also a spiritual heir to her mentor, the liberal hawk leader Madeleine Albright.

The hawkish orientation espoused by Kagan and Blinken was taken a step further by NATO's think tank, the Atlantic Council, which has advocated for nuclear brinkmanship. In February, Matthew Kroenig, the deputy director of the Atlantic Council's Scowcroft Center for Strategy and Security, argued for the consideration of the U.S.'s preemptive use of "tactical" nuclear weapons.[13]

From this small coterie of warmongers, one can easily detect the deep integration of two elite foreign affairs groups, both of which are the real drivers of the Ukraine crisis. The evolution of this crisis reveals the following set of tactics adopted by this belligerent clique:

- strengthening U.S. leadership over NATO, using the military alliance (rather than the UN) as the primary mechanism for foreign intervention;
- provoking a so-called adversary to war by refusing to rec-

ognize its claim to sovereignty and security over sensitive regions;
- planning the use of tactical nuclear weapons and conducting a "limited nuclear war" in or around the so-called adversary's territory; and
- imposing hybrid warfare in order to weaken and subvert the adversary through unilateral coercive measures and combining economic sanctions with financial, informational, propagandistic, and cultural measures along with a color revolution, cyberwarfare, lawfare, and other tactics.

If the desired results are achieved in Ukraine, the same strategy will undoubtedly be replicated in the Western Pacific.

Strategic alignment does not mean that policy elites are not divided on other issues that they deem to be of lesser importance, such as climate change. Even on this matter, however, the United States is demanding that Europe stop importing natural gas from Russia. John Kerry, Biden's climate envoy, is noncommittal about the potential negative environmental impacts of such a move, in part because the United States wants to replace Russian gas sales in Europe with its own.

In recent years, progressive forces around the world have launched several international campaigns to voice their concerns about the aggressive global strategy being pursued by the U.S., often using the term "New Cold War." However, the narratives put forth at times underestimate the depravity of some aspects of current U.S. foreign policy. The "Old Cold War" with the Soviet Union followed certain rules and bottom lines: the United States used a variety of political and economic means to exert pressure and seek to subvert the Soviet state, and the two sides acknowledged one another's scope of interests and security needs. However, the U.S. did not try to change the national boundaries of nuclear adversaries. This is not the case today, as seen by the *Wall Street Journal*'s open declaration that the United States should demonstrate its ability to win a nuclear war, a stance which is undergirded by the foreign policy elite's claim that Ukraine and Taiwan must be protected as they are both strategic locations within the Western military perimeter.[14] Even the Cold War leader Kissinger has expressed concern and opposition to current U.S. foreign policy, arguing that the correct strategy is to divide China and Russia and warning that there will be dangerous consequences if the U.S. directly pursues war against these two nuclear-armed states simultaneously.

The U.S. Bourgeoisie Prepares for War Against China

Washington has sought to economically decouple the United States from China through trade and technology wars, a process that was initiated by the Trump administration and has continued under Biden's leadership. However, this policy has spurred unintended consequences. On the one hand, due to the formation of global supply chains, U.S. and European manufacturing industries rely heavily on imports from China, and Biden has faced domestic opposition with calls to scale back trade war tariffs in order to ease the enormous pressure of inflation in the United States. On the other hand, although China did not initiate economic decoupling, the pressure of the trade and technology wars has promoted the development of the "internal grand circulation" within the country (reducing reliance on exports and relying more on domestic consumption). Since the pandemic, there has been a superficial phased increase in the trade of merchandise between the U.S. and China.

It must be noted, however, that there is a change underway in the basic logic of U.S. relations with China: the U.S. bourgeoisie has been tightening its alliance against China and supporting the bellicose strategy of Washington. This situation stems from both economic and ideological factors. For one, GDP figures of the U.S. and other countries in the West mask the contributions made by labor in factories in the Global South. For example, Apple's highly profitable sales in the United States appear in the U.S.'s GDP numbers, but the actual source of their high returns is the surplus created by the massively efficient and low-cost advanced productive labor force in Shenzhen, Chongqing, and other cities in China where Foxconn factories are located.[15] China has come a long way from the era of large factories with low-paid unskilled workers and has developed an extremely sophisticated industrial, logistical, and societal infrastructure that, as of 2019, accounted for 28.7 percent of global manufacturing.[16] Moving the whole supply chain from China to India or Mexico would be a decades-long process and cannot be based on just lower wages.

Few sectors of the U.S. economy depend heavily on the local Chinese market for sales, with U.S. chipmakers being the exception. Major firms such as Boeing, Caterpillar, General Motors, Starbucks, Nike, Ford, and Apple (at 17 percent) obtain less than 25 percent of their revenue from China.[17] The total revenue of S&P 500 companies is $14 trillion, no more than 5 percent of which is related to sales inside China.[18] U.S. CEOs are unlikely to oppose the direction of U.S. foreign policy on China, as they are not being presented with a clear path to increase their long-term access to China's growing internal market. This attitude was on display during Disney's May 2022 earnings call when CEO Bob Chapek expressed confidence in the company's success even without access to China's market.[19] This approach toward China is visible across key U.S. industries:

TECH/INTERNET. Nine of the top ten richest Americans are in the tech/internet industry, the zeitgeist of our time, with the partial exception of Elon Musk, the CEO of the electric automobile manufacturer Tesla, whose first pot of gold also came from the internet industry. Compared to the lists of the richest Americans from past decades, those from traditional sectors such as manufacturing, banking, and oil have been overtaken by a rising tech elite, which is steeped in anti-China attitudes due to the difficulties they have faced in penetrating the Chinese market. U.S. tech giants such as Google, Amazon, and Facebook have virtually no market in China, while companies like Apple and Microsoft face increasing difficulties. In the past decade, the Chinese technology and telecommunications corporation Huawei surpassed Apple in terms of market share within China, only for Apple to regain the top spot due to U.S. sanctions, which banned the sale of semiconductor chips—a key component in smartphones—to Huawei. The Chinese government is reportedly embracing indigenous Linux and Office Productivity systems to replace Microsoft Windows and Office software. Traditional IT companies such as IBM, Oracle, and EMC (collectively referred to as IOE) have long been marginalized in the Chinese market by the Alibaba-driven de-IOE wave, which seeks to replace IBM servers, Oracle databases, and EMC storage devices with indigenous and open-source solutions. U.S. tech giants yearn for a change to the political system in China that would open the door to the country's massive market, and major actors in this sector are actively working to advance Washington's hostile foreign policy. Eric Schmidt, the former CEO and executive chairman of Google, led the establishment of the U.S. government's Defense Innovation Unit in 2016 and the National Security Commission on Artificial Intelligence in 2018. His fervent promotion of the "China Threat" theory reflects the prevailing opinion of the U.S. tech community, which also shapes public discourse. Twitter and Facebook have partnered with U.S. and Western governments to increasingly censor criticisms of their foreign policy and influence discussion around key issues—such as the pandemic, Hong Kong, and Xinjiang—in the name of combatting disinformation campaigns allegedly launched by China and other so-called adversaries.

MANUFACTURING. U.S. manufacturing remains dependent on Chinese production capacity. Consistent investment and technological innovation in U.S. manufacturing were effectively abandoned during the neoliberal period, and, despite Obama's and Trump's calls to near-shore manufacturing back to North America, little has been accomplished in this regard. However, U.S. manufacturing investments in China have decreased in recent years, with the notable exception of Tesla's mega-factory in Shanghai. Even in this case, however, it is important to note that Elon Musk has won numerous U.S. government and military procurement contracts through his space exploration firm SpaceX, whose Starlink satellite system was criticized by China for its "close encounters" with the Chinese space station on two occasions in 2021. The Chinese People's Liberation Army warned that the U.S. may seek to militarize the Starlink system. The deployment of Starlink's services in Ukraine during the war is evidence of this dynamic. Musk's potential acquisition of Twitter would be unlikely to change the company's relationship with U.S. and Western governments and orientation toward China and Russia.

FINANCE. The U.S. financial services industry has long expected China's capital markets to open further to them, their ultimate hope being regime change in China that would lead the country to an outright neoliberal path. The anti-Chinese attitude of the influential Hungarian-born U.S. financial magnate and philanthropist George Soros is well known. In January 2022, Soros tweeted that "China's Xi Jinping is the greatest threat that open societies face today."[20] These comments came after Jamie Dimon, the CEO of JPMorgan

Chase, declared in November 2021 that the multinational bank would outlive the Communist Party of China (though he later apologized for this comment and said he was joking). Dimon also implied that China would suffer a heavy military strike if it attempted to reunify Taiwan, a threat for which he made no apology.[21] This hostile attitude is a response to the fact that China's capital markets are not advancing in the direction that Wall Street would prefer, as evidenced by the Chinese government strengthening capital controls and delisting a series of Chinese stocks from the U.S. stock exchange. At the investing conglomerate Berkshire Hathaway's annual shareholders meeting for 2022, Charlie Munger, vice chairman of the company, stated that China was still "worth" the investment. Even in this case, however, Munger accepted the premise of his interviewer, who characterized the Chinese government as an "authoritarian regime" that commits "human rights violations." For Munger, China is only worth the extra risk because one can invest in better businesses at lower prices.

RETAIL AND CONSUMER SECTORS. U.S. retail and consumer industries have long been squeezed by their Chinese competitors. In March 2021, Nike and other companies boycotted Xinjiang cotton on the false grounds of forced labor. Shortly thereafter, Nike released an advertisement that was criticized for promoting racist stereotypes about Chinese people, resulting in a further loss of its market share, which had already begun to be outflanked by the Chinese brand Anta.

Furthermore, there is a significant disconnect between the two countries' cultural and entertainment industries, with domestically produced movies accounting for 85 percent of the Chinese box office in 2021. Marvel superhero movies, once popular among Chinese filmgoers, have been unable to enter the Chinese market due to ideological concerns, with zero box office takings in China in 2021. The recent Marvel production *Doctor Strange in the Multiverse of Madness* yet again features anti-Chinese scenes, including a reference to the far-right, anti-government newspaper *The Epoch Times*. It has not been screened in China. These cases reflect U.S. companies' trade-offs between commercial interests—reaching the Chinese consumer market—and political ideology—opposing the Chinese political system.

The U.S. Military-Industrial Complex and the Drive for War

The U.S. military-industrial complex plays a special role in galvanizing cooperation between strategic economic, technological, political, and military sectors toward imperialist interests. In 2021, the top six military contractors in the world—Lockheed Martin, Boeing, Raytheon Technologies, BAE Systems, Northrop Grumman, and General Dynamics—had combined sales of over $128 billion to the U.S. government.[22] Big Tech companies including Amazon, Microsoft, Google, Oracle, IBM, and Palantir (founded by the extremist Peter Thiel) have formed close bonds with the U.S. military, signing thousands of contracts worth tens of billions of dollars in recent decades.[23] The tech industry plays the strategic role of collecting data in the vast U.S. intelligence empire and is at the center of U.S. soft-power media and social media hegemony, ensuring digital domination over the majority of the Global South. As such, this sector has become immune from meaningful regulation or threats of de-monopolization.

The U.S. drive for military supremacy leads to spending sprees in the areas of weapons, computer technology (silicon chips, in particular), advanced communications (including satellite cyber warfare), and biotechnology. The U.S. government has officially requested $813 billion for the military as part of its 2023 budget (which does not factor in additional military spending that is disguised in other sections of the overall budget), and the Pentagon claims it will need at least $7 trillion in appropriations over the next ten years.[24]

The privatization of the state under neoliberalism has led to the development of a revolving door between the U.S. government and the private sector over the past four decades. The state has become a vehicle for high level government officials including congresspersons, senators, policy and security advisors, cabinet members, colonels, generals, and presidents from both parties to become multi-millionaires by leveraging their political insider status with private interest groups.[25] Within governmental bureaucracy, the phrase "national security" opens the spigot for personal and corporate greed and radical military expansion even wider. Under this prevalent form of First World, legalized corruption, firms often tender payoffs to officials after they leave public office. These legal bribes are essentially payments in arrears for services granted while in office. For example, upon leaving office, former public officials are frequently hired as paid employees, board members, or advisors with the same firms that they had previously advocated on behalf of, provided favorable voting for, or awarded government contracts to as public officials.[26] Some prominent examples of this pervasive dynamic include the following:

- Bill Clinton claims to have been $16 million in debt when he left the White House in 2001, but, by 2021, he was worth an estimated $80 mllion.[27]
- With shocking impunity, at least 85 of the 154 people from private interest groups who met or had phone conversations scheduled with Hillary Clinton while she led the State Department under President Obama donated a combined $156 million to the Clinton Foundation.[28]
- James "Mad Dog" Mattis, a retired four-star general,

former secretary of defense under Trump, and former board member of CNAS, had a net worth of $7 million in 2018, five years after his "retirement" from the military. This was earned through significant payments from a wide list of military contractors and included $600,000 to $1.25 million in stock and options in the major defense contractor General Dynamics.[29]

- Lloyd Austin, the secretary of defense under President Biden, formerly served on the board of directors of several military-industrial companies such as United Technologies and Raytheon Technologies. Austin earned the majority of his $7 million net worth after "retiring" as a four-star general.[30]

Between 2009 and 2011, over 70 percent of top U.S. generals worked for military contractors after retiring from their position. Generals also double dip by simultaneously receiving compensation from the Pentagon and payments from private military contractors.[31] In 2016 alone, nearly 100 U.S. military officers went through the revolving door between the government and private military contractors, including 25 generals, 9 admirals, 43 lieutenant generals, and 23 vice admirals.[32]

During the Trump administration, many Obama-era officials moved to the private sector, consulting and advising the world's largest corporations, only to return to the White House under Biden. In a staggering display of this revolving door, the Biden administration has appointed more than 15 senior officials from the corporate consultancy firm WestExec Advisors, which was founded in 2017 by a team of former Obama administration officials and claims to provide "unparalleled geopolitical risk analysis" to its clients (including "Managing China-Related Risk in an Era of Strategic Competition").[33] The firm facilitates cooperation between Big Tech and the U.S. military, with clients including Boeing,

Palantir, Google, Facebook, Uber, AT&T, the drone surveillance company Shield AI, and the Israeli artificial intelligence firm Windward. WestExec alumni working in the Biden administration include Secretary of State Blinken, Director of National Intelligence Avril Haines, Deputy Director of the CIA David Cohen, Assistant Secretary of Defense for Indo-Pacific Security Affairs Ely Ratner, and former White House press secretary Jen Psaki.[34]

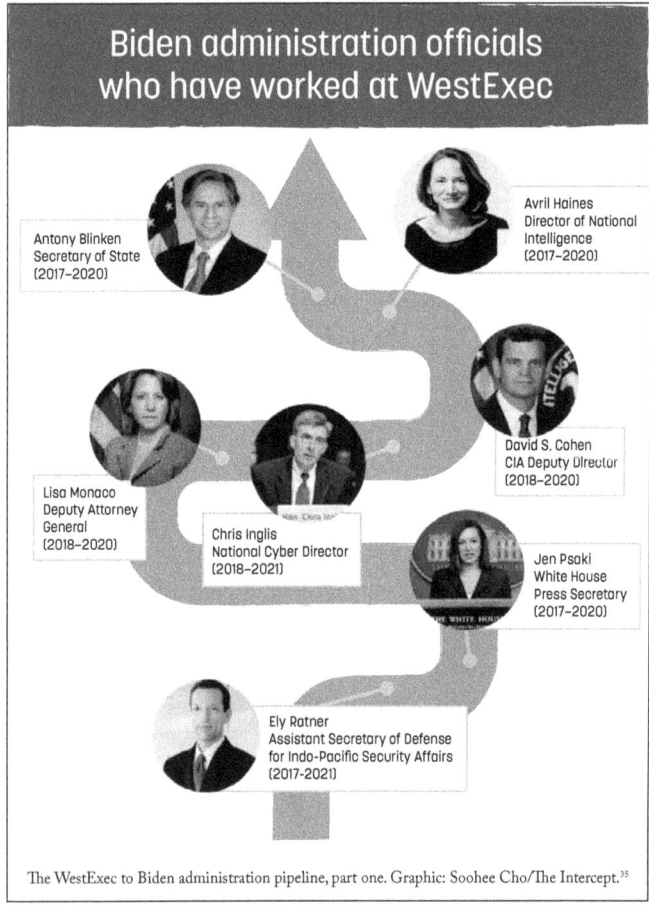

The WestExec to Biden administration pipeline, part one. Graphic: Soohee Cho/The Intercept.[35]

The Weakening of Domestic Resistance to U.S. Militarism

In 1973, the United States abolished military service conscription, or what was known as the draft, after which the U.S. military cleverly and misleadingly referred to itself as an all-volunteer army. This was done to reduce domestic opposition to U.S. wars abroad, especially from the children of propertied and middle-class families who had become vocal against the U.S. war of aggression in Vietnam. Although the measure was justified in the name of selecting more professional and dedicated soldiers, in reality, the bourgeoisie sought to prey upon the economic vulnerabilities of poorer working-class families, who they recruited into service through offers of technical training and secure earnings. Technological advances in warfare allowed the United States to simultaneously increase its capacity to kill civilians and enemy combatants in invaded countries while reducing the death rate of U.S. soldiers. For example, in the $2.2 trillion war against Afghanistan between 2001 and 2021, only 2,442—1 percent—of the 241,000 people killed (including over 71,000 civilians) were U.S. military personnel.[35] The reduction in U.S. death tolls has weakened the domestic emotional connection to U.S. war campaigns, which has further been blunted by the rise of private military contractors. By the mid-2010s, it was estimated that nearly half of the U.S. armed forces in Iraq and Afghanistan were employed by private military contractors.[36] In 2016, the world's largest private military contractor, ACADEMI (initially founded by Erik Prince as Blackwater) was purchased by the world's largest private equity firm, Apollo, for an estimated $1 billion.[37] Far from an all-volunteer army, today, it is increasingly apt to describe the U.S. military as an all-mercenary army.

The United States is further emboldened in its warmongering by the fact that, while it has invaded or participated in military operations in over a hundred countries, it has never been invaded or experienced large-scale civilian casualties at the hands of foreign governments. The psychology of U.S. exceptionalism is shaped by the fact that the current generation of political elites largely grew up after the end of the Cold War, a period defined as the so-called "end of history," when their country appeared to be invincible. The United States had not experienced a serious challenger either abroad or at home until the rise of China. As a result, this elite is particularly ahistorical in its worldview, seized by delusions of grandeur, and consequently feels unconstrained—an extremely dangerous combination.

The military-industrial complex, composed of generals, politicians, tech companies, and private military contractors, is pursuing a massive expansion of U.S. military capacity. Today, nearly all in Washington use China as well as Russia as their pretext for this build up. Meanwhile, many of them have committed or supported war crimes in Iraq, Afghanistan, Syria, Libya, and elsewhere.

Few influential individual capitalists in the United States are willing to openly stand against the chorus demonizing China, and those who do are disciplined or ostracized. One rarely comes across publicly dissenting views or calls for restraint in the op-ed sections of the *New York Times* or the *Wall Street Journal*. During the 2020 presidential campaign, Michael Bloomberg was heavily criticized for being "soft" on China after he stated that the Communist Party was responsive to the public and refused to label President Xi Jinping as a dictator. Bloomberg appears to have been successfully disciplined; under the Biden administration, he joined the war hysteria and was named chair of the Pentagon's Defense Innovation Board in February 2022. The global management consulting firm McKinsey & Company, which has favored greater economic engagement with China, has faced increasing criticism for these views, being smeared by the *New York Times* as "help[ing] raise the stature of authoritarian and corrupt governments across the globe."[38] Consequently, McKinsey's influence in U.S. business circles has been greatly weakened. Though a small number of figures—such as Ray Dalio, billionaire investor and founder of Bridgewater Associates—continue to express optimism about U.S.-China relations, they are outliers.

More critically, those in the current upper echelon of the U.S. bourgeois elite have diversified their investments across a slew of industries, enabling them to overcome the narrow, short-term economic interests of any one industry and to align with the "big picture" of U.S. strategy. In contrast to millionaires of generations past who were focused on a single industry, the billionaires of today have developed a more shared consciousness and can envision the major long-term returns from a fully liberalized Chinese market that would follow the overthrow of the Chinese state. Consequently, these billionaires are motivated to support the U.S. containment of China despite the short-term losses they might suffer as a result. As detailed above, this big bourgeoisie funds a large swathe of think tanks and policy groups through non-profit foundations, shaping U.S. policy discussions and proposals.

Among the upper-middle-class elite, there is a small group of far-right libertarian isolationists mainly composed of intellectuals and represented by the Cato Institute. This political network speaks out against the U.S. Federal Reserve System and foreign intervention and is opposed to the U.S.'s role in Ukraine. However, it is marginalized in the U.S. foreign policy arena and does not wield much influence.

As Karl Marx once noted, capitalists have always been a "band of warring brothers." This band maintains a modern state that has a massive, permanent body of armed men and women, intelligence functionaries, and spies. In 2015, 4.3 million individuals in the United States had security clearance to access "confidential," "secret," or "top secret" government material.[39] Regardless of any electoral result, this state apparatus is ultimately able to exert its dominance and guide U.S. foreign policy, as evidenced during the Trump administration's inability to implement its own foreign policy.

The Rise of the Far Right and the False Nature of Checks and Balances in the U.S. Political System

The hostility of the U.S. ruling bourgeois elite and middle classes toward China has deep, racist roots. Trump's four years in office coincided with the formation of a united coalition of populist and white supremacist right-wing movements known as the Alt-Right. Stephen Bannon, a mouthpiece of this movement, is a former chairman of the white supremacist website *Breitbart News Network* and is unsurprisingly one of the most active anti-China campaigners in the United States. The Alt-Right's support base comes from the lower middle class: mostly white people with annual household incomes of around $75,000. While Bannon and even Trump himself like to boast of the support they get from "the white working class," their primary support base is in fact the lower middle class—not the working class.

The Republican Party has benefited electorally from the creation of this neofascist voting bloc. The Alt-Right tends to lionize big capitalist personalities and desires upward mobility to join the elite. Meanwhile, this bloc expresses hatred toward both elitist political and cultural leaders for blocking their road to wealth as well as toward the working class. In 1951, the prominent U.S. sociologist C. Wright Mills offered the following characterization of the U.S. middle classes:

> They are rear guarders. In the shorter run, they will follow the panicky ways of prestige; in the longer run, they will follow the ways of power, for, in the end, prestige is determined by power. In the meantime, on

the political marketplace . . . the new middle classes are up for sale; whoever seems respectable enough, strong enough, can probably have them. So far, nobody has made a serious bid.[40]

The Trump administration directed the lower middle class's resentment of their deteriorating economic situation toward China. The U.S. economy has never fully recovered from the subprime mortgage crisis of 2008, when loose monetary policy enabled big capitalists to reap enormous profits while the working class and the lower middle class suffered great losses. The latter group, angry and frustrated with their situation and in dire need of a spokesperson, was mobilized by Trump to become his key vote bank with the help of white supremacy, racial capitalism, and a New Cold War to suppress China as an opponent in an all-out manner.

Today, hostility toward China has become widespread across the U.S. population. The impression that China is the arch enemy of the free world and the greatest threat to the United States has been emphatically reinforced by mainstream media outlets and internet platforms, while freedom of speech for those who oppose this dangerous trend has been increasingly restricted. Any acknowledgment of Russian and Chinese perspectives or criticism of U.S. foreign policy toward these countries meets strong public criticism. Public opinion in the United States increasingly resembles the McCarthyist period of the 1950s and, in certain ways, the social climate bears disturbing similarities to that of Germany in the early 1930s.

Outsiders often misunderstand the real nature of checks and balances and the separation of powers in the U.S. political system. Unlike the history of European constitutional reforms that were spawned by social revolutionary movements, the U.S. Constitution, which was originally founded by a group of property holders (including slaveholders), was designed from the beginning to protect the rights of private property owners against what they feared could become mob majoritarian rule. To this day, the Constitution allows for the dismantling of most traditional bourgeois social and legal rights.

Measures such as the electoral college, which was originally implemented to protect the interests of southern slave-holding and other smaller rural states, were designed to impede the people's direct vote for president (one person, one vote). This undemocratic system, which is safeguarded by a difficult and onerous process to amend the Constitution, resulted in both Bush Jr. and Trump winning the presidency despite receiving fewer votes than their respective opponents. Despite the eventual extension of voting rights to Black people, women, and those without property, voter disenfranchisement continues to this day. As of 2021, 19 states had enacted a total of 34 voter suppression laws that could limit the voting rights of up to 55 million voters in those states.[41] Meanwhile, the unelected Supreme Court has the power to overturn voting rights legislation, strike down affirmative action, and allow religious organizations to abridge civil rights.

A 2010 Supreme Court ruling known as *Citizens United* removed limits on private and corporate contributions to elections, making them a contest of financial strength.[42] In the 2020 elections, overall spending for the presidential, congressional, and Senate races was $14 billion.[43] In addition to financial competition, there is also psychological-technological competition: the persuasive technological tools based on social media, behavioral economics, and Big Data play a huge role in shaping electoral processes. At the same time, these tools are extremely expensive, helping to ensure that politics is a near exclusive game for the rich. In 2015, the median wealth of U.S. senators exceeded $3 million.[44] This is hardly a government that is checked and balanced by the people.

Are We Doomed to War?

In 2014, Xi Jinping, shortly after becoming China's top leader, told then U.S. President Obama that "the broad Pacific Ocean is vast enough to embrace both China and the United States."[45] Rejecting this diplomatic olive branch, then U.S. Secretary of State Hillary Clinton boasted in a private speech that the United States could call the Pacific "the American Sea" and threatened to "ring China with missile defense."[46] In 2020, the UK's Center for Economics and Business Research (CEBR) predicted that China would overtake the United States to become the world's largest economy by 2028, a threshold that haunts the U.S. elite. U.S. foreign policy and public opinion in recent years have fixated on preparations to wage a hot war to contain China before that can take place. The proxy war in Ukraine can be seen as a prelude to this hot war. The ideological mobilization to prepare for war is already in full swing in the United States. The wheels of neofascism are turning, and a new era of McCarthyism has arisen. So-called democratic politics are only a cover for the rule of the bourgeois elite; they will not serve as a braking mechanism for the war machine.

There are 140 million working and poor people in the United States, with 17 million children suffering from hunger—six million more than before the pandemic.[47] While a portion of this class does express ideological support for U.S. warmongering policy, this support directly contradicts their interests: the near trillion-dollar military budget comes at the expense of providing funding to guarantee healthcare, education, infrastructure, and other human rights, as well as combating climate change. Historically, progressive groups in the United States such as Black and feminist movements have had a strong spirit of anti-war struggle, and leaders such as Dr. Martin Luther King, Jr. and Malcolm X courageously fought to build a wave of domestic resistance to U.S.

aggression in Southeast Asia. Sadly, today, some (but not all) progressive leaders in the United States have been unwilling to challenge Washington's anti-China campaign or, worse, have even become supporters of it.

There are important moral voices in the United States that speak out. However, it must be noted that the few progressive groups opposed to a New Cold War have been vilified for allegedly justifying genocide in Xinjiang. The U.S. political system ruthlessly works to marginalize voices from this section of society.

Although the United States and its allies are aggressively pursuing global military expansion through NATO, the vast majority of the world does not welcome their war making. On March 2, 2022, the UN General Assembly held the 11th emergency special session, and countries which together constitute more than half of the world's population voted against or abstained from voting on the draft resolution titled "Aggression against Ukraine." Meanwhile, countries which represent 85 percent of the world's population have not endorsed the U.S.-led sanctions against Russia.[48] Washington's attempts to escalate and prolong the war and to force a decoupling of Moscow and Beijing will lead to massive economic dislocation, which will bring about sizeable negative reactions to U.S. rule. Even countries like India and Saudi Arabia are deeply concerned about the excesses of the United States in freezing Russian foreign exchange reserves and reinforcing the hegemony of the dollar. Similarly, the presidents of Mexico, Bolivia, Honduras, El Salvador, and Guatemala did not attend the Summit of the Americas hosted by the United States in Los Angeles in June 2022 because of the exclusion of Cuba, Venezuela, and Nicaragua. Resistance to U.S. rule is growing in Latin America. It should be noted, however, that international platforms such as the UN are not actually capable of restraining the United States from waging wars. Washington refuses to be bound by anything but its own rules-based international order.

In the United States, the Biden administration is providing massive military aid to Ukraine to create a protracted war to weaken Russia to the maximum extent possible and bring about regime change. It is also deviating from the spirit of the three Sino-U.S. joint statements and destabilizing the Taiwan Strait in various ways. Though the United States does have great military power, its current economic strength, while immense, is in a perpetual state of decline and crisis.

As John Ross shows in this study, U.S. economic supremacy is waning and may be ended by the Chinese economic juggernaut. In addition, the United States, along with its NATO allies, face multiple profound economic and ecological difficulties. The U.S.-driven war will exacerbate these problems. The war may doom Europe to lower, possibly negative GDP growth, along with inflation and increased and socially useless military spending. The United States has effectively abandoned any pretense of a serious strategy to address climate change, not to mention that its unending pursuit of war has exacerbated the climate catastrophe. And, ironically, despite the domestic political consensus for economic decoupling, U.S. firms continue to increase orders to China—substantive decoupling remains a pipe dream.

The United States will not just collapse economically, however; Washington's drive for war, sanctions, and economic decoupling will continue to damage its own economy and jeopardize the world food supply chain. The resulting global social instability will, in turn, further weaken the U.S. economy and generate even more challenges to its rule, including growing opposition to the hegemony of the dollar.

China's relatively stable social governance, strong national defense, diplomatic strategy of peace, and resistance to succumbing to U.S. power can, as Chinese State Councilor Yang Jiechi put it, allow the country to proceed "from a position of strength" and eventually force the United States to give up the illusion that it could go to war with China and win.[49] It is in the interests of the Global South that China remain a strong socialist, sovereign state and that it continue to promote alternative policies for global governance such as the concept of "building a community with a shared future for humanity" and the Global Development Initiative. There must be an immediate commitment to reinvigorating viable multilateral projects of the Global South such as BRICS and the Non-Aligned Movement, initiatives in which much of the world shares a common interest. The world population, the vast majority of which is located in the Global South, must resist war and call for peace. The United States is not the first empire to overreach with arrogance and hubris, and it, too, will eventually see its power come to an end.

"Notes on Exterminism" for the Twenty-First-Century Ecology and Peace Movements

JOHN BELLAMY FOSTER

In 1980, the great English historian and Marxist theorist E. P. Thompson, author of *The Making of the English Working Class* and leader of the Movement for European Nuclear Disarmament, wrote the pathbreaking essay "Notes on Exterminism, the Last Stage of Civilization."[1] Although the world has undergone a number of significant changes since, Thompson's essay remains a useful starting point in approaching the central contradictions of our times, characterized by the planetary ecological crisis, COVID-19 pandemic, New Cold War, and current "empire of chaos"—all arising from features deeply embedded in the contemporary capitalist political economy.[2]

For Thompson, the term *exterminism* referred not to the extinction of life itself, since some life would remain even in the face of a global thermonuclear exchange, but rather to the tendency toward the "extermination of our [contemporary] civilization," understood in its most universal sense. Nevertheless, exterminism pointed to mass annihilation and was defined as consisting of those "characteristics of society—expressed in differing degrees, within its economy, its polity, and its ideology—which thrust it in a direction whose outcome must be the extermination of multitudes."[3] "Notes on Exterminism" was written eight years before climatologist James Hansen's famous 1988 testimony on global warming to the U.S. Congress and the formation that same year of the UN Intergovernmental Panel on Climate Change. Hence, Thompson's treatment of exterminism focused squarely on nuclear war and did not directly address the other emerging exterminist tendency of contemporary society: the planetary ecological crisis. Yet, his perspective was a deeply socioecological one. The tendency toward exterminism in modern society was thus seen as directly opposed to "the imperatives of human ecological survival," demanding a worldwide struggle for a socially egalitarian and ecologically sustainable world.[4]

With the demise of the Soviet Union and the end of the Cold War in 1991, the nuclear threat that had loomed over the planet since the Second World War seemed to subside. As a result, most subsequent considerations of Thompson's exterminism thesis have considered it primarily in the context of the planetary ecological crisis, itself a source of "the extermination of multitudes."[5] However, the advent of the New Cold War over the last decade has brought the threat of nuclear holocaust back into the center of world concerns. The 2022 Ukraine War, the origins of which date back to the 2014 U.S.-engineered Maidan coup and the resulting Ukrainian Civil War fought between Kyiv and the breakaway republics of the Russian-speaking Donbass region in Ukraine, has now evolved into a full-scale war between Moscow and Kyiv. This took on an ominous worldwide significance on February 27, 2022, with Russia, three days into its military offensive in Ukraine, placing its nuclear forces on high alert as a warning against a direct NATO intervention in the war, whether by non-nuclear or nuclear means.[6] The potential for a global thermonuclear war between the leading nuclear powers is now greater than at any time in the post–Cold War world.

It is therefore necessary to address these dual exterminist

tendencies: both the planetary ecological crisis (including not only climate change but also the crossing of the eight other key planetary boundaries that scientists define as essential for the Earth's ability to be a safe home for humanity) and the growing threat of global nuclear annihilation. In approaching the dialectical interconnections between these two global existential threats, emphasis must be placed on updating the historical understanding of the thrust toward nuclear exterminism as it metamorphosed in the decades of U.S. unipolar power, while the world's attention was directed elsewhere. How is it that the threat of global thermonuclear war is once again hanging over the globe, three decades after the end of the Cold War and at a time when the risk of irreversible climate change looms on the horizon? What approaches need to be adopted within the peace and environmental movements to counter these interrelated global existential threats? To answer these questions, it is important to address such issues as the nuclear winter controversy, the counterforce doctrine, and the U.S. quest for global nuclear supremacy. Only then can we perceive the full dimensions of the global existential threats imposed by today's catastrophe capitalism.

Nuclear Winter

In 1983, teams of atmospheric scientists in both the United States and the Soviet Union produced models appearing in the major scientific journals predicting that a nuclear war would lead to a "nuclear winter." This took place in the midst of the Ronald Reagan administration's nuclear buildup, associated with the Strategic Defense Initiative (better known as Star Wars) and the growing threat of nuclear Armageddon. The outcome of a global thermonuclear exchange resulting in megafires in a hundred or more cities, it was discovered, could enormously reduce the average temperature of the Earth by pushing soot and smoke into the atmosphere and blocking solar radiation. The climate would be altered much more abruptly and in the opposite direction from global warming, introducing rapid global cooling causing temperatures to drop by several degrees or even "several tens of degrees" Celsius across the world (or at least across the hemisphere) in a matter of a month, with horrific consequences for life on Earth. Thus, although hundreds of millions—perhaps even a billion or more people—would be killed by the *direct* effects of a global thermonuclear exchange, the *indirect* effects would be far worse, annihilating most people on the planet via starvation—even those not caught up in the direct effects of nuclear firebombs. The nuclear winter thesis had a powerful effect on the nuclear arms race that was taking place at the time and played a role in getting the U.S. and Soviet governments to pull back from the brink.[7]

However, the power elite in the United States saw the nuclear winter model as a direct attack on the nuclear armaments industry and the Pentagon, aimed at the Star Wars program in particular. It therefore led to one of the biggest scientific controversies of all time, despite the fact that the controversy was more political than scientific, since the scientific results were never really in doubt. Although claims were made that the initial nuclear winter models from NASA scientists were too simple and that studies were produced pointing to effects less extreme than originally envisioned—"nuclear autumn" rather than nuclear winter—the nuclear winter thesis was validated again and again by scientific models.[8]

Nevertheless, if the initial response of the public and political leaders to the nuclear winter studies helped to create a strong movement to dismantle nuclear weapons, contributing to nuclear arms control and the end of the Cold War, this was soon countered by powerful military, political, and economic interests behind the U.S. nuclear war machine. Thus, the corporate media together with political forces launched various campaigns meant to discredit the nuclear winter thesis.[9] In 2000, the popular science magazine *Discover* went so far as to list nuclear winter as one of its "20 Greatest Scientific Blunders in the Last 20 Years." Yet, the most that *Discover* could claim in this respect was that the key scientists behind the most influential nuclear winter study in the 1980s had pulled back by 1990, claiming that the average temperature reduction as a result of a global nuclear exchange was estimated to be somewhat smaller than originally conceived and would at most constitute a 36°F (20°C) *drop* in average temperature in the Northern Hemisphere. This updated estimate, however, remained apocalyptic on a planetary level.[10]

In one of the greatest instances of denialism in the history of science, surpassing even the denial of climate change, the public sphere and the military widely rejected these scientific findings on nuclear winter out of hand based on the charge that the original estimate had somehow been "exaggerated." The exaggeration charge has been used in ruling circles for decades, up to the present, to downplay the full effects of nuclear war. In the case of Pentagon capitalism, such denial was clearly motivated by the reality that, if the scientific results on nuclear winter were allowed to stand, the strategic planning aimed at fighting a "winnable" nuclear war, or at least one in which one's own side would "prevail," would be senseless. Once the atmospheric effects are considered, the global devastation cannot be confined to a particular nuclear theater; the unimaginable effects would, within several years of the global thermonuclear exchange, destroy all but a tiny fraction of the population of the Earth, going beyond what was even envisioned by mutual assured destruction (MAD).

In some ways, the catastrophic effects of nuclear war have always been downplayed by nuclear planners. As Daniel Ellsberg points out in *The Doomsday Machine*, the estimated death toll from all-out nuclear warfare that U.S. strategic analysts provided was a "fantastic underestimate" from the start, "even before the discovery of nuclear winter," since they deliberately omitted the firestorms in cities resulting from nuclear blasts—the largest impact on the overall urban population—on the questionable grounds that the level of devastation was too difficult to estimate.[11] As Ellsberg writes:

> Yet even in the sixties the firestorms caused by thermonuclear weapons were known to be predictably the *largest* production of fatalities in a nuclear war. . . . Moreover, what no one would recognize . . . [until the first nuclear winter studies emerged some twenty-one years after the Cuban Missile Crisis] were the indirect effects of our planned first strike that gravely threatened the other two thirds of humanity. These effects arose from another neglected consequence of our attacks on cities: smoke. In effect, in ignoring fire, the [Joint] Chiefs [of Staff] and their planners ignored that where there's fire there's smoke. But what is dangerous to our survival is not the smoke from ordinary fires, even very large ones—smoke that remained in the lower atmosphere and soon would be rained out—but smoke propelled into the upper atmosphere from the *firestorms* that our nuclear weapons were sure to create in the cities we targeted.
>
> Ferocious updrafts from these multiple firestorms would loft millions of tons of smoke and soot into the stratosphere, which would not be rained out and would quickly encircle the globe, forming a blanket blocking most sunlight around the Earth for a decade or more. This would reduce sunlight and lower temperatures worldwide to a point that it would eliminate all harvests and starve to death—not all but nearly all—humans (and other animals that depend on

vegetation for food). The population of the Southern Hemisphere—spared nearly all direct effects from nuclear explosions, even from fallout—would be nearly annihilated, as would that of Eurasia (which the Joint Chiefs already foresaw, from direct effects), Africa and North America.[12]

Worse than the original pushback against the nuclear winter thesis, according to Ellsberg, writing in 2017, was the fact that, over the decades that followed, nuclear planners in the United States and Russia have "*continued* to include 'options' for detonating hundreds of nuclear explosions near cities, which would loft enough soot and smoke into the upper stratosphere to lead [via nuclear winter] to death by starvation of nearly everyone on Earth, including, after all, ourselves."[13]

The denialism built into the doomsday machine (the thrust to exterminism entrenched in Pentagon capitalism) is all the more significant given that not only were the original nuclear winter studies never disproven, but twenty-first-century nuclear winter studies, based on computer models more sophisticated than those of the early 1980s, have gone on to show that nuclear winter can be set off at lower levels of nuclear exchange than envisioned in the original models.[14] The importance of these new studies is symbolized by *Discover* magazine, which, in 2007—only seven years after it had included nuclear winter in its list of the twenty "greatest scientific blunders" of the previous two decades—carried an article entitled "The Return of Nuclear Winter," essentially repudiating its earlier piece.[15]

The most recent studies, motivated in part by nuclear proliferation, demonstrated that a hypothetical nuclear war between India and Pakistan fought with 100 fifteen-kiloton (Hiroshima-sized) atomic bombs could produce direct fatalities comparable to all deaths in the Second World War, in addition to the fatalities and suffering resulting from global famine in the longterm. The atomic explosions would immediately ignite firestorms of three to five square miles. Burning cities would release some five million tons of smoke into the stratosphere, circling the Earth within two weeks, which could not be removed by rainfall and might remain for more than a decade. By blocking sunlight, this would decrease food production globally by 20 to 40 percent. The stratospheric smoke layer would absorb warming sunlight, heating the smoke to temperatures near water's boiling point, resulting in an ozone layer reduction of 20 to 50 percent near populated areas and generating UV-B increases unprecedented in human history, such that fair-skinned individuals could get severe sunburns in around six minutes and levels of skin cancer would go off the charts. Meanwhile, it is estimated that up to 2 billion people would die of famine.[16]

The new series of nuclear winter studies, published in major peer-reviewed scientific journals beginning in 2007 and continuing to the present, did not stop there. They also looked at what would happen if there were a global thermonuclear exchange involving the five leading nuclear powers: the United States, Russia, China, France, and the United Kingdom. The United States and Russia alone, which account for most of the world's nuclear arsenal, have thousands of strategic nuclear weapons with an explosive power ranging from seven to eighty times that of the Hiroshima bomb (although some thermonuclear weapons developed in the 1950s and '60s that have since been discontinued were a thousand times as powerful as the atom bomb). A single strategic nuclear weapon hitting a city would ignite a firestorm covering a surface area of 90 to 152 square miles. Scientists calculated that the fires from a full-scale global thermonuclear exchange would propel into the stratosphere 150 to 180 million tons of black carbon soot and smoke that would remain for twenty to thirty years and would prevent up to 70 percent of solar energy from reaching the Northern Hemisphere and up to 35 percent with respect to the Southern Hemisphere. The noonday sun would end up looking like a full moon at midnight. Global average temperatures would fall below freezing every day for one or two years, or even longer in the main agricultural regions of the Northern Hemisphere. Average temperatures would dip below those experienced in the last Ice Age. The growing seasons of agricultural areas would disappear for more than a decade, while rainfall would decrease by up to 90 percent. Most of the human population would die of starvation.[17]

In his 1960 book *On Thermonuclear War*, RAND Corporation physicist Herman Kahn presented the notion of the "doomsday machine," which would kill everyone on Earth in the event of a nuclear war.[18] Kahn did not advocate building such a machine, nor did he contend that either the United States or the Soviet Union had done so or were then seeking to do so. He merely suggested that a mechanism that would ensure no survivability from nuclear war would be a cheap alternative with which to achieve complete and irrevocable deterrence on all sides and take nuclear warfare off the table. As Ellsberg, himself a former nuclear strategist, has since remarked—in line with scientists Carl Sagan and Richard Turco, who helped develop the nuclear winter model—today's strategic arsenals in the hands of the dominant nuclear powers, if detonated, constitute an actual doomsday machine. Once set in motion, the doomsday machine would almost certainly directly or indirectly annihilate most of the population on the planet.[19]

Counterforce and the U.S. Drive to Nuclear Primacy

From the 1960s, when Moscow achieved rough nuclear parity with Washington, until the demise of the Soviet Union, the dominant nuclear strategy during the Cold War between the United States and the Soviet Union was based on the notion of Mutually Assured Destruction (MAD). This principle, which refers to the possibility of utter devastation on both sides, including the deaths of hundreds of millions of people, effectively translates into nuclear parity. However, as nuclear winter studies indicate, the consequences of an all-out nuclear war would go far beyond even this, extending to the destruction of almost all human life (as well as most other species) on the entire planet. Still, ignoring the nuclear winter warnings, the United States, with far more resources than the Soviet Union, sought to transcend MAD in the direction of U.S. "nuclear primacy" so as to restore the level of U.S. nuclear preeminence of the early Cold War years. *Nuclear primacy*, as opposed to *nuclear parity*, means "eliminating the possibility of a retaliatory strike" and thus is also referred to as "first strike capability."[20] In this respect, it is significant that Washington's official defense posture has consistently included the possibility of the United States carrying out a first strike nuclear attack on nuclear or non-nuclear states.

In addition to introducing the doomsday machine concept, Kahn, as one of the leading U.S. strategic planners, also coined the key terms *countervalue* and *counterforce*.[21] *Countervalue* refers to targeting an enemy's cities, civilian population, and economy and is aimed at complete annihilation, thus leading to MAD. *Counterforce*, in contrast, refers to targeting the enemy's nuclear weapons facilities to prevent retaliation.

When the counterforce strategy was originally introduced by Robert McNamara, the U.S. defense secretary in John F. Kennedy's administration, it was seen as a "no cities" strategy that would attack the opponent's nuclear weapons rather than civilian populations, and it has sometimes been fallaciously justified in those terms since. McNamara, however, soon realized the flaws in the counterforce strategy, namely that it provokes a nuclear arms race directed at achieving (or denying) nuclear primacy. Moreover, the notion that a "preemptive" counterforce strike did not involve attacks on cities was incorrect from the start, as targets included nuclear command centers in cities. He therefore abandoned the effort shortly after in favor of a nuclear strategy based on MAD, which he saw as the only true approach to nuclear deterrence.[22]

This U.S. nuclear strategy prevailed for most of the 1960s and '70s and was characterized by the acceptance of rough nuclear parity with the Soviet Union and thus of the possible reality of MAD. However, this broke down in the final year of the Jimmy Carter administration. In 1979, Washington strong-armed NATO into allowing nuclear-armed cruise and Pershing II missiles, both counterforce weapons aimed at the Soviet nuclear arsenal, to be sited in Europe, a decision that ignited the European antinuclear movement.[23] In the subsequent U.S. administration under Ronald Reagan, Washington adopted the counterforce strategy in full force.[24] The Reagan administration introduced Star Wars, aimed at developing a comprehensive antiballistic missile system capable of defending the U.S. homeland. Though this was subsequently abandoned as impractical, it nonetheless led to other antiballistic missile systems in later administrations.[25] In addition, under the Reagan administration the United States pushed the MX missile (which later became known as the Peacemaker), viewed as a counterforce weapon able to destroy Soviet missiles before they were launched. All of these weapons threatened the "decapitation" of Soviet forces in a first attack as well as the ability to intercept through antiballistic missile systems what few Soviet missiles survived.[26] Counterforce weapons required greater accuracy since they were no longer conceived as city-busters as in "countervalue" attacks, but rather as precision targeting of hardened missile silos, mobile land-based missiles, nuclear submarines, and command-and-control centers. It was here, in counterforce weapons, that the United States had a technological advantage.

This major nuclear arms buildup, beginning in 1979 with the planned deployment in Europe of missile delivery systems carrying nuclear warheads, generated the great nuclear war protests of the 1980s in Europe and North America as well as Thompson's critique of exterminism and scientific research about nuclear winter. Nevertheless, today, "counterforce remains the sacrosanct principle of American nuclear strategy," aimed at nuclear primacy, in the words of Janne Nolan of the Arms Control Association.[27]

With the dissolution of the Soviet Union in 1991 and the end of the Cold War, Washington immediately commenced the process of translating its new unipolar position into a vision of permanent U.S. supremacy over the entire globe, beginning with the February 1992 *Defense Policy Guidance* issued by then Undersecretary of Defense Paul Wolfowitz.[28] This was to be enacted through a geopolitical expansion of the areas of Western dominance to regions formerly part of the Soviet Union or within its sphere of influence in order to thwart the reemergence of Russia as a great power. At the same time, in a climate of nuclear disarmament and with the deterioration of the Russian nuclear force under Boris Yeltsin, the United States sought to "modernize" its nuclear weapons, replacing them with more technologically advanced strategic weaponry with the object not of enhancing deterrence, but rather of achieving nuclear primacy.[29]

The U.S. pursuit of nuclear primacy in the post–Cold War world by continuing to promote counterforce weapons was known as the "maximalist" strategy in debates over nuclear policy at the time and was opposed by those who advocated for a "minimalist" strategy that relied on MAD. In the end, the maximalists won and the New World Order came to be defined by both the enlargement of NATO, with Ukraine seen as the ultimate geopolitical and strategic pivot, and by the U.S. pursuit of a maximalist goal of absolute nuclear dominance and first strike capability.[30]

In 2006, Keir A. Lieber and Daryl G. Press published the landmark article "The Rise of U.S. Nuclear Primacy" in *Foreign Affairs*, the flagship journal of the Council on Foreign Relations. In their article, Lieber and Press argued that the United States was "on the verge of attaining nuclear primacy," or first strike capability, and that this had been its aim since at least the end of the Cold War. As they put it, "the weight of evidence suggests that Washington is, in fact, deliberately seeking nuclear primacy."[31]

What placed such first strike capability seemingly within Washington's reach was the new nuclear weaponry associated with nuclear modernization that, if anything, accelerated after the Cold War. Weapons such as nuclear-armed cruise missiles, nuclear submarines able to fire their missiles near the shore, and low-flying B-52 stealth bombers carrying both nuclear-armed cruise missiles and nuclear gravity bombs could more effectively penetrate Russian or Chinese defenses. More accurate intercontinental ballistic missiles could fully eliminate hardened missile silos. Improved surveillance could allow for the tracking and destruction of mobile land-based missiles and nuclear submarines. Meanwhile, the more accurate Trident II D-5 missiles being introduced on U.S. nuclear submarines carried larger-yield warheads to use on hardened silos. More advanced remote sensing technology in which the United States has had the lead has greatly enhanced its ability to detect mobile land-based missiles and nuclear submarines. The ability to target the satellites of other nuclear powers could weaken or eliminate their capacity to deliver nuclear missiles.[32]

The siting of strategic weapons in countries recently admitted to NATO and near or on Russian borders would serve to enhance the speed with which nuclear weapons could strike Moscow and other Russian targets, giving the Kremlin no time to react. The Aegis ballistic missile defense facilities that the United States established in Poland and Romania are also potential offensive weapons capable of launching nuclear-armed tomahawk cruise missiles.[33] Nuclear missile defense facilities, mainly useful in the case of countering retaliation to a first strike by the United States, could shoot down a limited number of missiles that had survived and were launched on the other side, but these anti-ballistic missile systems would be ineffective in the face of a first attack since they would be overwhelmed by the sheer number of missiles and decoys. Furthermore, in recent decades, the United States has developed large numbers of high-precision, *non-nuclear* aerospace weapons to be used in a counterforce strike aimed at enemy missiles or command-and-control facilities that are comparable to nuclear weapons in their counterforce effects due to precision targeting based on satellites.[34]

According to Lieber and Press, writing in 2006, "the odds that Beijing will acquire a survivable nuclear deterrent in the next decade are slim," and the survivability of the Russian deterrent was in question in the face of a massive U.S. first strike. "What our analysis suggests is profound: Russia's leaders can no longer count on a survivable nuclear deterrent." As they wrote, the United States was "seeking primacy in every dimension of modern military technology, both in its conventional arsenal and in its nuclear forces," something known as "escalation dominance."[35]

The signing of the New Strategic Arms Reduction Treaty, or New START, between the United States and Russia in 2010, while limiting nuclear weapons, did not prevent a race toward the modernization of counterforce weapons that would allow one side to destroy the other side's armaments. The signing of the New START Treaty between the United States and Russia in 2010, while limiting nuclear weapons, did not prevent a race toward modernization of counterforce weapons to destroy the other side's weapons. In fact, the limits on numbers of nuclear weapons permitted made a counterforce strategy, in which the United States had the upper hand, much more feasible, since one of the three primary bases for survivability of a nuclear retaliatory arsenal (along with hardening of land-based missile sites and concealment) is the sheer number and thus redundancy of such weapons.[36] With nuclear primacy as the goal set in Washington, the United States began unilaterally to withdraw from some of the main nuclear treaties established in the Cold War. In 2002, under the George W. Bush administration, the United States unilaterally withdrew from the Anti-Ballistic Missile Treaty. In 2019, under the Donald Trump administration, Washington withdrew from the Intermediate-Range Nuclear Forces Treaty, claiming that Russia had violated it. In 2020, again under Trump, the United States withdrew from the Open Skies Treaty (which placed limits on reconnaissance flights over other countries); this was followed by Russia's withdrawal in 2021. There is little doubt that withdrawal from these treaties was favorable to Washington by allowing it to expand its counterforce options in its quest for nuclear primacy.

Given the U.S.'s pursuit of overall nuclear dominance, Russia has attempted to modernize its nuclear weapon systems over the last two decades, though it is at a distinct disadvantage in terms of counterforce capability. Its fundamental nuclear strategy is therefore determined by fears of a U.S. first strike that could effectively eliminate its nuclear deterrent and its ability to retaliate. Thus, it has strived to reestablish a credible deterrent. As Cynthia Roberts of the Saltzman Institute of War and Peace at Columbia University wrote in "Revelations About Russia's Nuclear Deterrence Policy" in 2020, Russians perceive further U.S. improvements to strategic forces, both conventional and nuclear, as part of a continuous effort to "stalk Russia's nuclear deterrent and deny Moscow a viable second-strike option," effectively eliminating its nuclear deterrent altogether through "decapitation."[37] While the

United States has adopted a maximum nuclear "defense" posture of threatening "nuclear first use and phased escalation" in which it retains dominance at every level of escalation, this compares to Russia's approach of "all-out war once deterrence fails" while continuing to rely primarily on MAD.[38]

However, in recent years, Russia and China have leaped ahead in strategic weapons technology and systems. In order to counter Washington's attempts to develop first strike capability and neutralize its nuclear deterrents, both Moscow and Beijing have turned to asymmetrical strategic weapons systems designed to counterpoise U.S. superiority in missile defense and high-precision targeting. Intercontinental ballistic missiles are vulnerable because, while they reach hypersonic speeds—usually defined as Mach 5, or five times the speed of sound or greater—when they reenter the atmosphere, they follow an arc that constitutes a predictable ballistic path, like a bullet. They thus lack surprise; their targets are predictable, and they can theoretically be intercepted by antiballistic missiles. Hardened missile silos housing intercontinental ballistic missiles are also distinct targets and today are far more vulnerable given both nuclear and non-nuclear U.S. high-precision, satellite-guided missiles. Confronted with these counterforce threats to their basic deterrents, Russia and China have pushed ahead of the United States in developing hypersonic missiles that can maneuver aerodynamically in order to dodge missile defenses and prevent the adversary from knowing the ultimate intended target. Russia has developed a hypersonic missile called the Kinzhal that is reputed to reach Mach 10 or more on its own and another hypersonic weapon, Avangard, that, boosted by a rocket, can reach the astounding speed of Mach 27. China has a "waverider" hypersonic cruise missile that reaches Mach 6. Borrowing from Chinese folklore, it is referred to as an "assassin's mace," a weapon effective against a much better-armed adversary.[39] Russia and China, meanwhile, have been developing antisatellite "counterspace" weapons designed to remove the U.S. advantage of high-precision nuclear and non-nuclear weapons.⁴⁰

So-called nuclear primacy has remained just beyond Washington's grasp given the technological prowess of the other leading nuclear powers. Moreover, a nuclear arms race spurred by a counterforce strategy is fundamentally irrational, threatening a global thermonuclear conflagration with consequences far greater than even those envisioned by the MAD scenario, with its hundreds of millions of deaths on both sides. Nuclear winter means that, in a global nuclear exchange, *the entire planet* would be engulfed by the smoke and soot circling the stratosphere, killing off almost all of humanity.

Given this reality, the U.S. nuclear posture, which is based on the notion of prevailing in an all-out nuclear war, is particularly dangerous since it denies the role of firestorms in cities and thereby the effects of smoke that would loft up into the upper atmosphere and blot out most of the sun's rays. The search for nuclear primacy, therefore, leads from MAD to madness.⁴¹ As Ellsberg writes:

> The hope of successfully avoiding mutual annihilation by a decapitating attack has always been as ill-founded as any other. The realistic conclusion would be that a nuclear exchange between the United States and the Soviets [Russians] was—and is—virtually certain to be an unmitigated catastrophe, not only for the two parties but for the world. . . . [Policymakers] have chosen to act as if they believed (and perhaps actually do believe) that such a threat is not what it is: a readiness to trigger global omnicide.⁴²

The New Cold War and the European Theater

In "Notes on Exterminism" and his general stance as a leader of the Movement for European Nuclear Disarmament in the

1980s, Thompson argued that the nuclear arms buildup in Europe taking place at the time was a product of military machines and technological imperatives "tak[ing] place independently of the ebb and flow of international diplomacy, although it is given an upward thrust by each crisis or by each innovation by 'the enemy.'"[43] His argument was part of a strategy to unite the peace movements of the West and East against their respective establishments based on the premise that nuclear buildup was equally a product of both sides. However, in this regard, he belied his own evidence, which pointed to Washington's aggressive nuclear buildup of counterforce weapons and the placement of strategic weapons in Europe targeting the Soviet Union. In an article entitled "Nuclear Chicken" in the September 1982 issue of *Monthly Review*, Harry Magdoff and Paul M. Sweezy challenged this part of Thompson's argument, pointing not only to the strategic expansions of NATO under the United States, but also to the fact that the U.S. imperial order was heavily dependent on credible threats of first strikes directed at other countries, both nuclear and non-nuclear.[44]

In a 1981 introduction to the U.S. edition of *Protest and Survive* edited by Thompson and Dan Smith, Ellsberg listed a long series of documented instances beginning in 1949 in which the United States used threats of nuclear first strikes to pressure other countries (both nuclear and non-nuclear) to back down in order to achieve its imperial ends.[45] Between 1945 and 1996 alone, twenty-five cases of nuclear threats were documented, though others have occurred since.[46] In this sense, the use of nuclear warfare as a threat is built into U.S. strategy. The development of nuclear primacy through counterforce weapons held out the possibility that such threats could once again be credibly directed even at major nuclear powers such as Russia and China. Magdoff and Sweezy called this whole approach a game of "nuclear chicken," in which the United States was the most aggressive player.

Nuclear chicken did not end with the Cold War. The U.S. national security state, influenced by key figures such as Zbigniew Brzezinski, Carter's national security advisor and one of the principal architects of NATO's post–Cold War expansion, continued to seek ultimate U.S. geopolitical hegemony over Eurasia, which he referred as the "grand chessboard." Checkmate, according to Brzezinski, would constitute bringing Ukraine into NATO as a strategic nuclear alliance (though Brzezinski carefully excluded the nuclear aspect in presenting his geopolitical strategy), spelling the end of Russia as a great power and possibly leading to its breakup into various states, thereby marking U.S. supremacy over the entire globe.[47] This attempt to turn U.S. unipolar power after the Cold War into a permanent global empire required the expansion of NATO to the east, which commenced in 1997 during the Bill Clinton administration, gradually annexing to the Atlantic Alliance virtually all the countries between Western Europe and Ukraine, with the latter as the ultimate prize and a dagger at Russia's heart.[48] Here, there was a kind of oneness exhibited between the U.S.-directed strategy of expanding NATO and Washington's drive for nuclear primacy, which proceeded in almost lockstep.

The fact that Russia was compelled to consider the question of its own national security in the face of NATO's attempt to expand militarily into Ukraine should hardly surprise anyone. A decade into the expansion of NATO, which already encompassed eleven nations that were formerly either in the Warsaw Pact or part of the Soviet Union, and only a year after near U.S. nuclear primacy was highlighted in *Foreign Affairs*, Russian President Vladimir Putin startled the world by unequivocally declaring at the 2007 Munich Security Conference that "the unipolar model is not only unacceptable but impossible in today's world."[49] Nevertheless, consistent with its long-term strategy to extend into what Brzezinski had called the "geopolitical pivot" of Eurasia, thereby fatally weakening Russia, in 2008 NATO declared outright at its Bucharest Summit that it intended to bring Ukraine into the military-strategic (nuclear) alliance.

In 2014, the U.S.-engineered Maidan coup in Ukraine deposed the country's democratically elected president and imposed in his place a leader chosen by the White House, putting Ukraine in the hands of right-wing, ultra-nationalist forces. Russia's response was to incorporate Crimea into its territory following a popular referendum that gave the predominantly Russian-speaking Crimean population, who regarded themselves as independent and not part of Ukraine, a choice as to whether to remain in Ukraine or join with Russia. The coup (or "color revolution") led to Kyiv's violent repression of the populations in the Russian-speaking Donbass region of Ukraine, resulting in the Ukrainian Civil War between Kyiv (supported by Washington) and the breakaway Russian-speaking Donbass republics of Donetsk and Luhansk (supported by Moscow). The Ukrainian Civil War, which resulted in more than 14,000 deaths between 2014 and early 2022, continued at a low ebb over the following eight years despite the signing of the Minsk peace agreements in 2014, meant to end the conflict and give autonomy to the Donbass republics within Ukraine. In February 2022, Kyiv had massed 130,000 troops on the borders of Donbass in eastern Ukraine, firing on Donetsk and Luhansk.[50]

As the Ukrainian crisis worsened, Putin insisted on a number of Russia's red lines related to the country's essential security needs, consisting of:

1) adherence to the previous Minsk agreement (worked out by Russia, Ukraine, France, and Germany and signed onto by the Donbass people's republics and supported by the UN Security Council), thereby guaranteeing the autonomy and security of Donetsk and Luhansk,
2) an end to NATO's militarization of Ukraine, and

3) an agreement that Ukraine would remain outside of NATO.[51]

NATO, urged on by the United States, continued to cross all of these red lines, providing increased military aid to Kyiv in its war on the Donbass republics in what Russia interpreted as a de facto attempt to incorporate Ukraine into NATO.

On February 24, 2022, Russia intervened in the Ukrainian Civil War on the side of Donbass, attacking the Kyiv government's military forces. On February 27, Moscow put its nuclear forces on high alert for the first time since the end of the Cold War, confronting the world with the possibility of a global nuclear holocaust, this time between competing great capitalist powers. Figures in Washington, such as Senator Joe Manchin III (Democrat, West Virginia), have backed the idea of a U.S. imposition of a no-fly zone in Ukraine, which would mean shooting down Russian planes, in all probability escalating into a Third World War.[52]

Exterminism in Two Directions

It is common today to recognize that climate change represents a global existential threat that places the very survival of humanity in jeopardy. We are faced with a situation in which the continual expansion of capitalism based on the burning of ever larger amounts of fossil fuels points to the possibility—even probability, if the system of production is not altered radically in a matter of decades—of the downfall of industrial civilization, placing the survival of humanity in question. This is the meaning of environmental exterminism in our time. According to the UN Intergovernmental Panel on Climate Change (IPCC), net zero carbon dioxide emissions must be reached by 2050 if the world is to have a reasonable hope of keeping global average temperatures below a 1.5°C, or well below a 2°C, increase over preindustrial levels. Not to accomplish this is to invite the devastation of the Earth as a safe home for humanity and innumerable other species.

Climate change is part of a more general planetary ecological crisis associated with crossing the nine planetary boundaries, including those—beyond climate change itself—related to species extinction, stratospheric ozone depletion, ocean acidification, the disruption of the nitrogen and phosphorous cycles, the loss of ground cover/forests, declining fresh water sources associated with desertification, atmospheric aerosol loading, and the introduction of novel entities such as new synthetic chemicals and new genetic forms.[53] To this should be added the emergence of new zoonoses, as in the COVID-19 pandemic, resulting principally from the transformation of human beings' relationship to the environment, spurred by agribusiness.[54]

Yet, there is no doubt that climate change is at the center of the current global ecological crisis. Like nuclear winter, it poses a threat to civilization and the continuation of the human species. The IPCC tells us in its 2021–22 reports on the physical science of climate change and its impacts that the most optimistic scenario, though warding off irreversible climate change, is still one of growing global catastrophe in the decades ahead. Immediate action is required to protect the lives and living conditions of hundreds of millions, and perhaps billions, of people who will be exposed to extreme weather events of a kind that global civilization has never seen before.[55] To counter this requires the greatest movement of workers and peoples the world has ever seen in order to restore the conditions that allow for their existence, which have been usurped by the regime of capital, and to reestablish an ecologically sustainable world rooted in substantive equality.[56]

Ironically, the 2022 IPCC report, which was meant to draw the world's attention to the catastrophic nature of today's climate crisis, was published on February 28, 2022, four days after the Russian entry into the Ukrainian Civil War in defiance of NATO, resulting in growing concern over the possibility of a global thermonuclear exchange. Hence, the world's attention was drawn away from considering one global existential threat endangering all of humanity, *carbon omnicide*, by the sudden reemergence of another, *nuclear omnicide*.

As the world turned its attention to the possibility of war between the leading nuclear powers, the full planetary scale of the nuclear threat, as understood by science in terms of nuclear winter, was absent from the picture. Global warming and nuclear winter, though arising in different ways, are closely connected in climate terms, demonstrating that the world is on the brink of destroying most of the inhabitants of the Earth in one way or the other: global warming leading to a point of no return for humanity, and/or the death of hundreds of millions by nuclear fire, followed by days and months of global cooling (nuclear winter) and the extermination of most of the rest of the world's population through starvation. Just as the full destructive implications of climate change threatening the very existence of humanity are in large part denied by the powers that be, so are the full planetary effects of nuclear war, which scientific research about nuclear winter tells us will effectively annihilate the population of every continent on Earth. Furthermore, if global warming increases to the extent that global civilization is destabilized, something that natural scientists predict could happen if global average temperatures increase by 4°C, competition between capitalist nation-states will increase, thereby enhancing the risk of a nuclear conflagration and thus nuclear winter.[57]

Today, we are confronted with a choice between *exterminism* and the *human ecological imperative*.[58] The causal agent in the two global existential crises now threatening the human species is the same: capitalism and its irrational quest for exponentially increasing capital accumulation and imperial power in a limited global environment. The only possible response to this unlimited threat is a universal revolutionary movement rooted in both ecology and peace that turns away from the current systematic destruction of the Earth and its inhabitants and toward a world of substantive equality and ecological sustainability: namely, socialism.

Notes

What Is Propelling the United States into Increasing International Military Aggression?

1. Vyacheslav Tetekin, "How the US Pushed Ukraine into the War," Communist Party of the Russian Federation, April 4, 2022, https://cprf.ru/2022/04/how-the-us-pushed-ukraine-into-the-war/. The quotes and analysis in this section are from this source.
2. See Angus Maddison, *The World Economy: A Global Perspective* (Paris: Organisation for Economic Cooperation and Development, 2001). Note that other sources give the U.S. economy a much greater share of global GDP in 1950, with estimates in excess of 40 percent.
3. The data comparing the economic performance of the United States and China are taken from the IMF's database published accompanying the April 2022 *World Economic Outlook*, https://www.imf.org/en/Publications/WEO/weo-database/2022/April; U.S. Bureau of Economic Analysis, International Data, https://apps.bea.gov/iTable/iTable.cfm?ReqID=62&step=1#reqid=62&step=9&isuri=1&6210=4; *Trading Economics*, https://tradingeconomics.com/; World Bank, *World Development Indicators*, https://databank.worldbank.org/reports.aspx?source=world-development-indicators.
4. Federation of American Scientists, "Status of World Nuclear Forces," 2022, https://fas.org/issues/nuclear-weapons/status-world-nuclear-forces/.
5. Janan Ganesh, "The US will be the ultimate winner of Ukraine's crisis," *Financial Times*, April 5, 2022, https://www.ft.com/content/cd7270a6-f72b-4b40-8195-1a796f748c23.
6. "Events like This Happen Once a Century": Sergey Glazyev on the breakdown of epochs and changing ways of life, *The Saker*, 28 March 2022, https://thesaker.is/events-like-this-happen-once-

a-century-sergey-glazyev-on-the-breakdown-of-epochs-and-changing-ways-of-life/.
7. Micheal Clodfelter quoted in Edward Miguel and Gerard Roland, "The Long-run Impact of Bombing Vietnam," *Journal of Development Economics* 96 (1), 2011: 1–15. https://eml.berkeley.edu/~groland/pubs/vietnam-bombs_19oct05.pdf.
8. Edward Miguel and Gerard Roland, "The Long-run Impact of Bombing Vietnam," *Journal of Development Economics* 96 (1), 2011: 1–15. https://eml.berkeley.edu/~groland/pubs/vietnam-bombs_19oct05.pdf.

Who Is Leading the United States to War?

1. This article was originally written for a Chinese audience and adapted and published in *Guancha*, a Chinese news website.
2. *Meet the Press*, "War Game: What Would a Battle for Taiwan Look Like?," NBC News, May 15, 2022, https://www.nbcnews.com/meet-the-press/video/war-game-what-would-a-battle-for-taiwan-look-like-140042309777.
3. Center for a New American Security, "CNAS Supporters," accessed August 9, 2022, https://www.cnas.org/support-cnas/cnas-supporters.
4. Roxana Tiron, "U.S. Sees Rising Risk in 'Breathtaking' China Nuclear Expansion," *Bloomberg*, April 4, 2022, https://www.bloomberg.com/news/articles/2022-04-04/u-s-sees-rising-risk-in-breathtaking-china-nuclear-expansion.
5. North Atlantic Treaty Organization, "NATO 2022 Strategic Concept," June 29, 2022, https://www.nato.int/nato_static_fl2014/assets/pdf/2022/6/pdf/290622-strategic-concept.pdf.
6. Niall Ferguson, *Colossus: The Rise and Fall of the American Empire* (New York: Penguin Books, 2005).
7. Joan E. Greve, "Biden's Record Defense Budget Draws Progressive Ire Over Spending Priorities," *The Guardian*, April 3, 2022, https://www.theguardian.com/us-news/2022/apr/03/biden-record-defense-budget-progressive-spending-priorities; Alicia Parlapiano, Deborah B. Solomon, Madeleine Ngo and Stacy Cowley, "Where $5 Trillion in Pandemic Stimulus Money Went," *The New York Times*, March 11, 2022, https://www.nytimes.com/interactive/2022/03/11/us/how-covid-stimulus-money-was-spent.html.

8. Swiss Policy Research, "The American Empire and Its Media," March 2022, https://swprs.org/the-american-empire-and-its-media/; Laurence H. Shoup, *Wall Street's Think Tank: The Council on Foreign Relations and the Empire of Neoliberal Geopolitics, 1976–2019* (New York: Monthly Review Press, 2019); Richard Harwood, "Ruling Class Journalists," *The Washington Post*, October 30, 1993, https://www.washingtonpost.com/archive/opinions/1993/10/30/ruling-class-journalists/761e7bf8-025d-474e-81cb-92dcf271571e/.
9. Ivo H. Daalder and James M. Lindsay, "American Empire, Not 'If' but 'What Kind,'" *New York Times*, May 10, 2003, https://www.nytimes.com/2003/05/10/arts/american-empire-not-if-but-what-kind.html.
10. John Bellamy Foster, *Trump in the White House: Tragedy and Farce* (New York: Monthly Review Press, 2017).
11. Antony J. Blinken and Robert Kagan, " 'America First' Is Only Making the World Worse. Here's a Better Approach," *Brookings Institution*, January 4, 2019, https://www.brookings.edu/blog/order-from-chaos/2019/01/04/america-first-is-only-making-the-world-worse-heres-a-better-approach/.
12. Victoria Nuland, "Remarks at the U.S.-Ukraine Foundation Conference," *U.S. Department of State*, December 13, 2013, https://2009-2017.state.gov/p/eur/rls/rm/2013/dec/218804.htm.
13. Matthew Kroenig, "Washington Must Prepare for War with Both Russia and China," *Foreign Policy*, February 18, 2022, https://foreignpolicy.com/2022/02/18/us-russia-china-war-nato-quadrilateral-security-dialogue/.
14. Seth Cropsey, "The U.S. Should Show It Can Win a Nuclear War," *Wall Street Journal*, April 27, 2022, https://www.wsj.com/articles/the-us-show-it-can-win-a-nuclear-war-russia-putin-ukraine-nato-sarmat-missile-testing-warning-11651067733; "A Conversation with Representative Michael McCaul," *Council on Foreign Relations*, April 6, 2022, https://www.cfr.org/event/conversation-representative-michael-mccaul; Elliot Abrams, "The Ukraine War, China, and Taiwan," *Council on Foreign Relations*, May 3, 2022, https://www.cfr.org/blog/ukraine-war-china-and-taiwan.
15. John Smith, "The GDP Illusion: Value Added versus Value Capture," *Monthly Review* 64, no. 3 (July-August 2012), https://doi.

org/10.14452/MR-064-03-2012-07; Tricontinental: Institute for Social Research, "iPhone Workers Today Are 25 Times More Exploited Than Textile Workers in 19th Century England: The Thirty-Ninth Newsletter (2019)," September 25, 2019, https://thetricontinental.org/newsletterissue/iphone-workers-today-are-25-times-more-exploited-than-textile-workers-in-19th-century-england-the-thirty-ninth-newsletter-2019/.
16. Felix Richter, "China Is the World's Manufacturing Superpower," *Statista*, May 4, 2021, https://www.statista.com/chart/20858/top-10-countries-by-share-of-global-manufacturing-output/.
17. "10 US Companies with Highest Revenue Exposure to China," *Yahoo! Finance*, August 2, 2020, https://finance.yahoo.com/news/10-us-companies-highest-revenue-225350456.html.
18. Yardeni Research, Inc., *S&P 500 Revenues & the Economy*, June 13, 2022, https://www.yardeni.com/pub/stmktbriefrev.pdf; Office of the United States Trade Representative, "The People's Republic of China: U.S.-China Trade Facts," accessed August 9, 2022, https://ustr.gov/countries-regions/china-mongolia-taiwan/peoples-republic-china.
19. Phil Hall, "Can Marvel Films Profit without Playing in China? Here's What Disney CEO Bob Chapek Says," *Benzinga*, May 12, 2022, https://www.benzinga.com/general/entertainment/22/05/27166040/disneys-chapek-marvel-films-can-profit-without-playing-in-china.
20. George Soros (@georgesoros), "China's Xi Jinping is the greatest threat that open societies face today," Twitter, January 31, 2022, https://twitter.com/georgesoros/status/1488233860584427530?lang=en.
21. David Henry and Anshuman Daga, "Jamie Dimon jokes that JPMorgan will outlast China's Communist Party," *Reuters*, November 23 2021, https://www.reuters.com/business/jpmorgan-ceo-dimon-jokes-his-bank-will-outlast-chinas-communist-party-2021-11-23/.
22. Bloomberg Government, "The Top 10 Defense Contractors," June 10, 2021, https://about.bgov.com/top-defense-contractors/.
23. Big Tech Sells War, accessed August 9, 2022, https://bigtechsellswar.com/; April Glaser, "Thousands of Contracts Highlight Quiet Ties Between Big Tech and U.S. Military," *NBC News*, July 8, 2020, https://www.nbcnews.com/tech/tech-news/thousands-

contracts-highlight-quiet-ties-between-big-tech-u-s-n1233171; Joseph Nograles, "Buy PLTR Stock: Palantir Is a Defense Contractor Powerhouse," Nasdaq, October 14, 2021, https://www.nasdaq.com/articles/buy-pltr-stock%3A-palantir-is-a-defense-contractor-powerhouse-2021-10-14; Frank Konkel, "NSA Awards Secret $10 Billion Contract to Amazon," Nextgov, August 10, 2021, https://www.nextgov.com/it-modernization/2021/08/nsa-awards-secret-10-billion-contract-amazon/184390/.
24. Mike Stone, "Biden Wants $813 Billion for Defense as Ukraine Crisis Raises Alarm," *Reuters*, March 28, 2022, https://www.reuters.com/world/us/biden-wants-813-billion-defense-ukraine-crisis-raises-alarm-2022-03-28/; Michael A. Cohen, "Bloated Defense Budget Passes Easily but Congress Fights over Safety Net Programs," *MSNBC*, October 1, 2021, https://www.msnbc.com/opinion/bloated-defense-budget-passes-easily-congress-fights-over-safety-net-n1280568.
25. Open Secrets, accessed August 9, 2022, https://www.opensecrets.org/.
26. Ben Freeman, "The Hidden Costs of Star Creep: Generals Making More in Retirement Than in Service," *POGO: Project on Government Oversight*, February 8, 2012, https://www.pogo.org/analysis/2012/02/hidden-costs-of-star-creep-generals-making-more-in-retirement-than-in-service.
27. Sam DiSalvo, "How Much Is Bill Clinton Worth?" *Yahoo! News*, February 12, 2021, https://ca.news.yahoo.com/much-bill-clinton-worth-234218086.html.
28. CNBC, "Many Who Met with Clinton as Secretary of State Donated to Foundation," August 23, 2016, https://www.cnbc.com/2016/08/23/most-of-those-who-met-with-clinton-as-secretary-of-state-donated-to-foundation.html.
29. Jeremy Herb and Connor O'Brien, "Pentagon Pick Mattis Discloses Defense Industry Work," *Politico*, January 8, 2017, https://www.politico.com/blogs/donald-trump-administration/2017/01/james-mattis-defense-disclosures-233331.
30. Dan Alexander, "Here's How Much Secretary of Defense Lloyd Austin Is Worth," *Forbes*, June 18, 2021, https://www.forbes.com/sites/danalexander/2021/06/18/heres-how-much-secretary-of-defense-lloyd-austin-is-worth/?sh=552340be63e4.
31. Luke Johnson, "Report: 70 Percent of Retired Generals Took Jobs

with Defense Contractors or Consultants," *HuffPost*, November 20, 2012, https://www.huffpost.com/entry/defense-contractors-generals_n_2160771.
32. Tom Vanden Brook, Ken Dilanian, and Ray Locker, "How Some Retired Military Officers Became Well-Paid Consultants," *ABC News*, November 18, 2009, https://abcnews.go.com/Politics/retired-military-officers-retire-paid-consultants/story?id=9115368; Mandy Smithberger, "Brass Parachutes: The Problem of the Pentagon Revolving Door," *POGO: Project on Government Oversight*, November 5, 2018, https://www.pogo.org/report/2018/11/brass-parachutes.
33. Jonathan Guyer and Ryan Grim, "Meet the Consulting Firm That's Staffing the Biden Administration," *The Intercept*, July 6, 2021, https://theintercept.com/2021/07/06/westexec-biden-administration/; WestExec Advisors, accessed August 14, 2022, https://www.westexec.com/.
34. Jonathan Guyer and Ryan Grim, "Meet the Consulting Firm That's Staffing the Biden Administration," *The Intercept*, July 6, 2021, https://theintercept.com/2021/07/06/westexec-biden-administration/; Alex Thompson and Theodoric Meyer, "Janet Yellen Made Millions in Wall Street, Corporate Speeches," *Politico*, January 1, 2021, https://www.politico.com/news/2021/01/01/yellen-made-millions-in-wall-street-speeches-453223; Eric Lipton and Kennet P. Vogel, "Biden Aides' Ties to Consulting and Investment Firms Pose Ethics Test," *The New York Times*, November 28, 2020, https://www.nytimes.com/2020/11/28/us/politics/biden-westexec.html.
35. Neta C. Crawford and Catherine Lutz, "Human and Budgetary Costs to Date of the U.S. War in Afghanistan," *Costs of War Project*, April 15, 2021, https://watson.brown.edu/costsofwar/files/cow/imce/figures/2021/Human%20and%20Budgetary%20Costs%20of%20Afghan%20War%2C%202001-2021.pdf.
36. Bryan Stinchfield, "The Creeping Privatization of America's Armed Forces," *Newsweek,* May 28, 2017, https://www.newsweek.com/creeping-privatization-americas-forces-616347.
37. Ross Wilkers, "Apollo Group, Constellis Executives to Buy Out Security Services Contractor," *GovCon Wire*, August 15, 2016, https://www.govconwire.com/2016/08/apollo-group-constellis-executives-to-buy-out-security-services-contractor/.

38. Walt Bogdanich and Michael Forsythe, "How McKinsey Has Helped Raise the Stature of Authoritarian Governments," *The New York Times*, December 15, 2018, https://www.nytimes.com/2018/12/15/world/asia/mckinsey-china-russia.html.
39. Congressional Research Service, "Security Clearance Process: Answers to Frequently Asked Questions," October 17, 2016, https://crsreports.congress.gov/product/pdf/R/R43216.
40. C. Wright Mills, *White Collar: The American Classes* (New York: Oxford University Press, 1951), 353.
41. Tony Eskridge and Shailly Gupta Barnes, "Quick Facts on Voting Rights," *Kairos Center*, accessed August 9, 2022, https://kairoscenter.org/quick-facts-on-voting-rights/.
42. Ian Vandewalker, "Since *Citizens United*, a Decade of Super PACs," *The Brennan Center for Justice*, January 14, 2020, https://www.brennancenter.org/our-work/analysis-opinion/citizens-united-decade-super-pacs.
43. Brian Schwartz, "Total 2020 Election Spending to Hit Nearly $14 Billion, More than Double 2016's Sum," *CNBC*, October 28, 2020, https://www.cnbc.com/2020/10/28/2020-election-spending-to-hit-nearly-14-billion-a-record.html.
44. Dan Kopf, "The Typical US Congress Member Is 12 Times Richer than the Typical American Household," *Quartz*, February 12, 2018, https://qz.com/1190595/the-typical-us-congress-member-is-12-times-richer-than-the-typical-american-household/.
45. Embassy of the People's Republic of China in the United States, "Xi Jinping Holds Talks with President Barack Obama of the US," November 12, 2014, http://us.china-embassy.gov.cn/eng/zmgx/zxxx/201411/t20141115_4909273.htm.
46. William Gallo, "Clinton Says US Would 'Ring China with Missile Defense'," *Voice of America*, October 14, 2016, https://www.voanews.com/a/clinton-says-us-would-ring-china-with-missile-defense/3550418.html.
47. Shailly Gupta Barnes, "Explaining the 140 Million: Breaking Down the Numbers Behind the Moral Budget," *Kairos Center*, June 26, 2019, https://kairoscenter.org/explaining-the-140-million/; Save the Children, "Child Hunger in America," 2021, https://www.savethechildren.org/us/charity-stories/child-hunger-in-america.
48. No Cold War, "Briefing: The World Does Not Want a Global

NATO," July 28, 2022, https://nocoldwar.org/news/briefing-the-world-does-not-want-a-global-nato.

49. "China Says U.S. Cannot Speak from 'a Position of Strength'" *BBC News*, March 19, 2021, https://www.bbc.com/news/av/world-56456021.

"Notes on Exterminism" for the Twenty-First Century Ecology and Peace Movements

1. E. P. Thompson, "Notes on Exterminism, the Last Stage of Civilization," *New Left Review* 121 (1980): 3–31. Citations to this essay in the present article are taken from the slightly revised version in E. P. Thompson, *Beyond the Cold War* (New York: Pantheon, 1982), 41–79. See also E. P. Thompson et al., *Exterminism and the Cold War* (London: Verso, 1982); E. P. Thompson and Dan Smith, eds., *Protest and Survive* (New York: Monthly Review Press, 1981).
2. Thompson, *Beyond the Cold War*, 55; Samir Amin, *Empire of Chaos* (New York: Monthly Review Press, 1992).
3. Thompson, *Beyond the Cold War*, pp. 64, 73.
4. Thompson, *Beyond the Cold War*, 75–76.
5. Rudolf Bahro, *Avoiding Social and Ecological Disaster* (Bath: Gateway Books, 1994), 19–20; John Bellamy Foster, *Ecological Revolution* (New York: Monthly Review Press, 2009), 27–28; Ian Angus, *Facing the Anthropocene* (New York: Monthly Review Press, 2016), 178–81.
6. For a brief discussion of the events leading up the present Ukraine War, see The Editors, "Notes from the Editors," *Monthly Review* 73, no. 11 (April 2022).
7. Stephen Schneider, "Whatever Happened to Nuclear Winter?," *Climatic Change* 12 (1988): 215; Matthew R. Francis, "When Carl Sagan Warned About Nuclear Winter," *Smithsonian Magazine*, November 15, 2017; Carl Sagan and Richard Turco, *A Path Where No Man Thought: Nuclear Winter and the End of the Arms Race* (New York: Random House, 1990), 19–44.
8. Malcolm W. Browne, "Nuclear Winter Theorists Pull Back," *New York Times*, January 23, 1990.
9. Steven Starr, "Turning a Blind Eye Toward Armageddon—U.S. Leaders Reject Nuclear Winter Studies," *Public Interest Report* (Federation of American Scientists) 69, no. 2 (2016–17): 24.

10. Judith Newman, "20 of the Greatest Blunders in Science in the Last 20 Years," *Discover*, January 19, 2000.
11. Daniel Ellsberg, *The Doomsday Machine: Confessions of a Nuclear War Planner* (New York: Bloomsbury, 2017), 140. The failure to include the foremost cause of death from thermonuclear weapons directed at cities in the form of firestorms is deeply ingrained in the Pentagon. The declassified practical guide on nuclear weapons stockpile and management published by the U.S. Department of Defense for 2008 includes more than twenty pages on the effects of a nuclear weapons explosion in a city without a single mention of firestorms. See U.S. Department of Defense, *Nuclear Matters: A Practical Guide* (Washington: Pentagon, 2008), 135–58.
12. Ellsberg, *The Doomsday Machine*, 141–42.
13. Ellsberg, *The Doomsday Machine*, 18, 142.
14. Owen B. Toon, Allan Robock, and Richard P. Turco, "Environmental Consequences of Nuclear War," *Physics Today* (2008): 37–42; Alan Robock and Owen Brian Toon, *Local Nuclear War, Global Suffering* (New York: Scientific American, 2009).
15. Emily Saarman, "Return of Nuclear Winter," *Discover*, May 2, 2007.
16. Starr, "Turning a Blind Eye Toward Armageddon," 4–5; Alan Robock, Luke Oman, and Geeorgiy L. Stenchikov, "Nuclear Winter Revisited with a Modern Climate Model and Current Nuclear Arsenals: Still Catastrophic Consequences," *Journal of Geophysical Research* 112 (2007) (D13107): 1–14.
17. Starr, "Turning a Blind Eye Toward Armageddon," 5–6; Robock, Oman, and Stenchikov, "Nuclear Winter Revisited"; Joshua Coupe, Charles G. Bardeen, Alan Robock, and Owen B. Toon, "Nuclear Winter Responses to Nuclear War Between the United States and Russia in the Whole Atmosphere Community Climate Model Version 4 and the Goddard Institute for Space Studies Model E," *Journal of Geophysical Research: Atmospheres* (2019): 8522–43; Alan Robock and Owen B. Toon, "Self-Assured Destruction: The Climate Impacts of Nuclear War," *Bulletin of the Atomic Scientists* 68, no. 5 (2012): 66–74; Steven Starr, "Nuclear War, Nuclear Winter, and Human Extinction," Federation of American Scientists, October 14, 2015.
18. Herman Kahn, *On Thermonuclear War* (New Brunswick, NJ: Transaction Publishers, 2007), 145–51.

19. Ellsberg, *The Doomsday Machine*, 18–19; Sagan and Turco, *A Path Where No Man Thought*, 213–19. Here, the doomsday machine is not to be confused with the version of the doomsday machine in Stanley Kubrick's film *Dr. Strangelove*. Yet Kubrick's film drew on Kahn's notion and retains a concrete significance in the context of contemporary nuclear reality. See Ellsberg, *The Doomsday Machine*, 18–19.
20. Keir A. Lieber and Daryl G. Press, "The Rise of U.S. Nuclear Primacy," *Foreign Affairs* (2006), 44.
21. Sagan and Turco, *A Path Where No Man Thought*, 215.
22. John T. Correll, "The Ups and Downs of Counterforce," *Air Force Magazine*, October 1, 2005; Ellsberg, *The Doomsday Machine*, 120–23, 178–79.
23. Harry Magdoff and Paul M. Sweezy, "Nuclear Chicken," *Monthly Review* 34, no. 4 (September 1981): 4; Richard J. Barnet, "Why Trust the Soviets?," *World Policy Journal* 1, no. 3 (1984): 461–62.
24. Correll, "The Ups and Downs of Counterforce."
25. Steven Pifer, "The Limits of U.S. Missile Defense," Brookings Institution, March 30, 2015.
26. Cynthia Roberts, "Revelations About Russia's Nuclear Deterrence Policy," *War on the Rocks* (*Texas National Security Review*), June 19, 2020; Correll, "The Ups and Downs of Counterforce."
27. Janne Nolan, quoted in Correll, "The Ups and Downs of Counterforce."
28. "Excerpts from Pentagon's Plan: Preventing the Re-emergence of a New Rival," *New York Times*, March 8, 1992.
29. Lieber and Press, "The Rise of U.S. Nuclear Primacy," 45–48.
30. Richard A. Paulsen, *The Role of U.S. Nuclear Weapons in the Post-Cold War Era* (Maxwell Air Force Base, Alabama: Air University Press, 1994), 84; Michael J. Mazarr, "Nuclear Weapons After the Cold War," *Washington Quarterly* 15, no. 3 (1992): 185, 190–94; Zbigniew Brzezinski, *The Grand Chessboard* (New York: Basic Books, 1997), 46.
31. Lieber and Press, "The Rise of U.S. Nuclear Primacy," 43, 50.
32. Lieber and Press, "The Rise of U.S. Nuclear Primacy," 45.
33. Jack Detsch, "Putin's Fixation with an Old-School U.S. Missile Launcher," *Foreign Policy*, January 12, 2022; Jacques Baud (interview), "The Policy of USA Has Always Been to Prevent Germany and Russia from Cooperating More Closely," *Swiss Standpoint*,

March 15, 2022; Starr, "Turning a Blind Eye Toward Armageddon." Estonia has cruise missiles supplied by Israel: David Axe, "Estonia's Getting a Powerful Cruise Missile. Now It Needs to Find Targets," *Forbes*, October 12, 2021. Russia is also concerned with the possible reintroduction of Pershing II intermediate ballistic missiles in Europe.

34. Jaganath Sankaran, "Russia's Anti-Satellite Weapons: An Asymmetrical Response to U.S. Aerospace Superiority," Arms Control Association, March 2022.

35. Lieber and Press, "The Rise of U.S. Nuclear Primacy," 48–49, 52–53; Karl A. Lieber and Daryl G. Press, "The New Era of Counterforce: Technological Change and the Future of Nuclear Deterrence," *International Security* 41, no. 4 (2017). A key element of Beijing's nuclear deterrent is reducing the acoustic signature or noise level of its nuclear submarines. In 2011, it was believed that it would take China decades to reduce the acoustic signature of its submarines enough to survive a U.S. first strike. However, in less than a decade, China made significant advances toward that goal. Lieber and Press, "The New Era of Counterforce," 47; Caleb Larson, "Chinese Submarines Are Becoming Quieter," *National Interest*, September 10, 2020; Wu Riqiang, "Survivability of China's Sea-Based Nuclear Forces," *Science and Global Security* 19, no. 2 (2011): 91–120. The 2006 Lieber and Press article in *Foreign Affairs* resulted in criticisms of their analysis by both Russia and China, and also served to generate concerns in these states leading to the revival and modernization of their nuclear capabilities. Yet, the threat posed by the U.S. drive for nuclear primacy continues to stalk Russian and Chinese strategic planners. See Karl Lieber and Daryl G. Press, "Nuclear Weapons, Deterrence, and Conflict," *Strategic Studies Quarterly* 10, no. 5 (2016): 31–42.

36. Lieber and Press, "The New Era of Counterforce," 16–17.

37. Roberts, "Revelations About Russia's Nuclear Deterrence Policy"; Sankaran, "Russia's Anti-Satellite Weapons."

38. Alexey Arbatov, "The Hidden Side of the U.S.-Russian Strategic Confrontation," Arms Control Association, September 2016; Brad Roberts, *The Case for U.S. Nuclear Weapons in the 21st Century* (Stanford: Stanford University Press, 2015).

39. Richard Stone, "National Pride Is at Stake: Russia, China, United States Race to Build Hypersonic Weapons," *Science*, January

8, 2020, 176–96; Dagobert L. Brito, Bruce Bueno de Mesquita, Michael D. Intriligator, "The Case for Submarine Launched Non-Nuclear Ballistic Missiles," Baker Institute, January 2002.
40. Sankaran, "Russia's Anti-Satellite Weapons." The development of "countermeasure" strategies and technologies to elude counterforce attack on a nation's nuclear deterrence is emphasized by Russia and China, given the U.S. lead in counterforce. See Lieber and Press, "The New Era of Counterforce," 46–48.
41. See Diane Johnstone, "Doomsday Postponed?," in Paul Johnston, *From Mad to Madness: Inside Pentagon Nuclear War Planning* (Atlanta, GA: Clarity, 2017), 272–86.
42. Ellsberg, *The Doomsday Machine*, 307. Today, there is once again increased discussion in U.S. strategic circles of a "low-casualty" or "decapitation" first-strike capability on the part of the United States, which would seem to make nuclear firestorms less likely. See Lieber and Press, "The New Era of Counterforce," 27–32.
43. Thompson, *Beyond the Cold War*, 46.
44. Magdoff and Sweezy, "Nuclear Chicken," 3–6.
45. Daniel Ellsberg, "Introduction: Call to Mutiny," in Thompson and Smith, eds., *Protest and Survive*, i–xxviii. It was reprinted as "Call to Mutiny," *Monthly Review* 33, no. 4 (September 1981): 1–26.
46. Ellsberg, *The Doomsday Machine*, 319–22.
47. Brzezinski, *The Grand Chessboard*, 46, 92–96, 103.
48. Editors, "Notes from the Editors."
49. Diana Johnstone, "Doomsday Postponed?," 277.
50. Editors, "Notes from the Editors"; Diane Johnstone, "For Washington, War Never Ends," *Consortium News* 27, no. 76 (2022); John Mearsheimer, "On Why the West Is Principally Responsible for the Ukrainian Crisis," *Economist*, March 19, 2022.
51. Mark Episkopos, "Putin Warns the West to Heed Russia's Redlines in Donbass," *National Interest*, December 21, 2021; Associated Press, "Russia Publishes 'Red Line' Demands of U.S. and NATO Amid Heightened Tension Over Kremlin Threat to Ukraine," *Marketwatch*, December 18, 2021.
52. Luke Broadwater and Chris Cameron, "U.S. Lawmakers Say They Are Largely Opposed to a No-Fly Zone Over Ukraine," *New York Times*, March 6, 2022.
53. Will Steffen et al., "Planetary Boundaries: Guiding Human De-

velopment on a Changing Planet," *Science* 347, no. 6223 (2015): 736–46.
54. See Rob Wallace, *Dead Epidemiologists: On the Origins of COVID-19* (New York: Monthly Review Press, 2020).
55. UN Intergovernmental Panel on Climate Change, "Summary for Policymakers," *Climate Change 2022: Impacts, Adaption and Vulnerability* (Geneva: IPCC, 2022). See also "Summary for Policymakers," *Climate Change 2021*.
56. This conclusion is in fact consistent with the original scientists' assessment in the third part (on Mitigation) of the UN Intergovernmental Panel on Climate Change's *Sixth Assessment Report* (AR6). The scientists' assessment, *Summary for Policymakers* of AR6, part 3, was leaked in August 2021, months in advance of its final publication in April 2022. The published *Summary of Policymakers* of part 3 (known as the government assessment report) was severely censored and rewritten by governments, effacing the main findings on mitigation provided by scientists. See Editors, "Notes from the Editors," *Monthly Review* (June 2022), https://monthlyreview.org/2022/06/01/mr-074-02-2022-06_0/.
57. Ellsberg, *The Doomsday Machine*, 18.
58. Thompson, *Beyond the Cold War*, 76.

Ingram Content Group UK Ltd.
Milton Keynes UK
UKHW011422270323
419232UK00008B/91